P

The Great B....

"I dare you to read more than a chapter or two of *The Great Book of Journaling* without feeling compelled to put pen to paper or fingers to keyboard! This book is a beautiful quilt, each chapter written by one of the wisest voices in the journaling world, on every aspect of journal writing imaginable. That such journaling intelligence is accessible between two covers of one book is a gift to any existing or would-be journal keeper."

    —RUTH FOLIT, founder and past director of the International
      Association for Journal Writing

"I coach and accredit professional coaches and mentors, so I know what it takes for us to succeed personally and professionally. One of those success factors is having positive daily mental health and well-being practices. That's why I'm a fan of *The Great Book of Journaling*. It's a wonderful self-care resource for practicing what we preach to our clients, one that will help us and them live the lives we both desire."

    —DAWN CAMPBELL, business director, international authority for
      professional coaching and mentoring

"This is a GREAT BOOK for those who already journal and for those who are ready to journal! Every chapter is filled with ideas and examples that will spark your creative self into action! Buy a copy for yourself, and lots more for gifts!"

    —JOYCE CHAPMAN, author of *Journaling for Joy*

"As one of the 40 contributors to this book, I am excited by the collection's diverse approaches to journaling, all of them with something to teach me. This easy-to-engage-with collection offers strategies for journaling that will revive interest for long-time journal keepers and encourage new journal keepers to establish their journaling practice. Every chapter includes writing strategies that foster discovery as well as encouraging one to continue journaling for healing, for wisdom, and for capturing all of life's moments."

—SHEILA BENDER, founder of Writing It Real

The Great Book of Journaling is indeed great! The richness of the many journaling perspectives, benefits, and suggested journaling activities included makes this book a true gem. I highly recommend this book for new and avid journal writers alike who crave both inspiration and information to start, sustain, or deepen an existing journaling practice. This book will surely inspire you to pick up your pen and tap into your inner wisdom and well-being through journaling."

—REBECCA KOCHENDERFER, Journaling.com

"Journaling saved my life while battling a life-threatening illness. Never in the history of the world has there been a greater need for the in-depth introspection and self-healing that journal-keeping offers. *The Great Book of Journaling* is a stellar introduction to the joys and benefits of journaling by leaders in the field. Inspiration and guidance shine from every page."

—LUCIA CAPACCHIONE, art therapist, author, and originator of the Creative Journal Method

"What you'll find in *The Great Book of Journaling* is more than just a collection of ideas about journaling. Each of these chapters is meant to invite you deeper into a practice of listening to yourself, tuning into your intuition, and harnessing your natural powers to heal and create the life that you were meant to live. Ready for a fresh experience of the practice your therapist and every self-help book has been telling you to do? This book will touch your heart and help you connect with your inner creative self in a practice that can last the rest of your life!"

—JACOB NORDBY, author of *The Creative Cure–How Finding and Freeing Your Inner Artist Can Heal Your Life*

"Who wouldn't want a life of wellness, creativity, meaning, and purpose? As a psychotherapist who believes that my craft can be helpful in this respect, I must also acknowledge that journaling can also help get you there. You still have to put in the work, and you will want to learn from the best. I highly recommend T*he Great Book of Journaling*. It is full of practical wisdom, and it is a lot less expensive than therapy."

—JED DIAMOND, PhD, psychotherapist, author of *The Irritable Male Syndrome: Understanding and Managing the 4 Key Causes of Depression and Aggression*

"*The Great Book of Journaling*, which contains an eclectic variety of creative and meaningful ways to journal, serves as a valuable and practical guide to anyone interested in journaling. For those who already journal, the book invites the reader to explore new techniques and unlocks the key to the gifts of journaling."

—MERLE R. SAFERSTEIN, author of *Living and Leaving My Legacy*

The
GREAT BOOK
of
Journaling

The
GREAT BOOK
of
Journaling

How Journal Writing
Can Support
a Life of Wellness,
Creativity, Meaning
and Purpose

By Eric Maisel & Lynda Monk
Co-Editors

Conari Press

Coral Gables, FL

Cover Design: Ron Wheatley
Layout & Design: Carmen Fortunato

For permission requests, please contact the publisher at:
Mango Publishing Group
2850 S Douglas Road, 4th Floor
Coral Gables, FL 33134 USA
info@mango.bz

For special orders, quantity sales, course adoptions and corporate sales, please email the publisher at sales@mango.bz. For trade and wholesale sales, please contact Ingram Publisher Services at customer.service@ingramcontent.com or +1.800.509.4887.

The Great Book of Journaling: How Journal Writing Can Support a Life of Wellness, Creativity, Meaning and Purpose

Library of Congress Cataloging-in-Publication number: 2022933691
ISBN: (print) 978-1-64250-854-3, (ebook) 978-1-64250-855-0
BISAC category code SEL024000, SELF-HELP / Self-Management / Stress Management

Printed in the United States of America

For journal writers everywhere,
your story matters.

For Ann and Peter,
our supportive spouses.

Table of Contents

Eric's Introduction 12

Lynda's Introduction 14

1. Juicy Journaling by SARK 18

2. Journaling Basics by Mari L. McCarthy 26

3. Journaling Simplicity by Kathleen Adams 32

4. Journaling Resistance by Liz Crocker 40

5. The Reflective Journal by Lynda Monk 46

6. The Creative Journal by Lucia Capacchione 54

7. The Storytelling Journal by Judy Reeves 61

8. The Healing Journal by Jacob Nordby 67

9. The Legacy Journal by Merle R. Saferstein 74

10. The Elemental Journal by Midori Evans 80

11. The Digital Journal by Hannah Braime 87

12. The Planning Journal by Jennifer Britton 93

13. The Altered Journal by Chris Leischner 99

14. The Becoming Unstuck Journal by A M Carley 104

15. The Forest Journal by Mary Ann Burrows 110

16. The Audio Journal by Dwight McNair 117

17. The Conflict Resolution Journal by Linda Dobson 124

18. The Compassionate Journal by Ahava Shira 131

19. Contemplative Journaling by Kimberly Wulfert 138

20. Journaling as an Instrument of Mindfulness by Beth Jacobs 145

21. Journaling Your Transitions by Leia Francisco 151

22. The Writing Body by Emelie Hill Dittmer 157

23. Inner Critic Journaling by Emma-Louise Elsey 163

24. From Journal to Memoir by Eric Maisel 171

25. Keeping the Fragmentary Journal by Sheila Bender 178

26. Journaling in the Third Person by Lara Zielin 184

27. Journaling in Community by Mary Ann Moore 189

28. Journaling in a Group: A Facilitator's Perspective by Nancy Johnston 195

29. Journaling with Children by Nicolle Nattrass 201

30. Journals as Intergenerational Storytelling by Shehna Javeed 207

31. Journaling and Creative Writing by Diane Hopkins 214

32. Journaling and Design Inspiration by Meryl Cook 221

33. Journaling to Connect with Nature's Wisdom by Jackee Holder 226

34. Journaling and Traveling by April Bosshard 232

35. Journaling to Find Love by Kim Ades 239

36. Journaling and the Lost Words by Marisé Barreiro 245

37. Journaling for Personal Growth by Sandra Marinella 251

38. Journaling for Dream Fulfillment by Joyce Chapman 258

39. Journaling and the Pursuit of Happiness by Susan Borkin 264

40. Journaling for Your Future Self by Elena Greco 272

Conclusion 279

Acknowledgments 285

About the Authors 287

Eric's Introduction

By Eric Maisel

In a recent book of mine, *Redesign Your Mind*, I described how you can upgrade and redesign the source of your thoughts: your mind. In a second book, *The Power of Daily Practice*, I explained how daily practices help us live our life purposes and aid us in making daily meaning. In a third book, *Lighting the Way*, I introduced a contemporary philosophy of life based on self-awareness and personal responsibility. These three recent books have led me to this book, *The Great Book of Journaling*.

I wanted to co-edit this volume and introduce journaling to a wider audience because journaling can be your daily self-awareness practice. It can effectively support your intention to identify and live your life purposes, improve your indwelling style (the way you inhabit the room that is your mind), and help you solve personal and professional problems. It can be the go-to way you use your mind, maintain daily awareness, and take responsibility for your life. That's a lot!

Journaling is "just" a certain sort of conversation that you have with yourself. But what a "just"! Having that conversation is you taking the time to consciously stop amidst your hectic day and asking yourself:

- "What's on my mind?"
- "What's going on?"
- "What should I be aware of?

It is a conscious, intentional stopping, signaling that you intend to live wisely rather than blindly or impulsively. That you have done that stopping signals that you are on your own side and that you care about your own life. It is not about "doing a little writing." It is about your abiding and honorable commitment to yourself.

That's my view as to what journaling can mean and do. But, of course, there are many other views! This book presents a great variety of views, some of which do not necessarily speak to me personally. They may, however, speak to you! It is a tenet of my philosophy that I do not get to arbitrate the meaning in your life. You get to decide what's important and what's meaningful. For instance, it may move you deeply to connect up nature and journaling. Personally, I'd rather write in a bus station or a train station. But that's just me!

We have been through trying times individually, as a society, and as a world. Those trying times are continuing and will continue. We have ongoing epidemics of sadness, anxiety, loneliness, and isolation. The world has its enormous problems. Each individual is taxed to the limit and struggling to make sense of things. There is no "answer" to all of this—but there are responses that we can make.

We can take responsibility for our own thoughts and actions. We can put the world on our shoulders in our own small ways and lobby for justice, fairness, and goodness. We can love, give comfort, and occasionally smile. And we can endeavor to maintain courageous self-awareness by adopting practices that support that awareness. Journaling is one of those practices. It is not the only practice that you might adopt, but it is a great one.

I hope that the authors collected in this volume inspire you to find your own personal journaling practice. I think they will! Please enjoy—and, if you're moved to do so, please be in touch. You can always reach me at ericmaisel@hotmail.com. Good luck!

Lynda's Introduction

By Lynda Monk

Eric Maisel and I know first-hand the incredible value of journaling. Together, with the contributors in this book, we wanted to create a collection that would shine a bright light on the bounty of goodness that journaling can bring into peoples' lives. The result is the book you are holding now, *The Great Book of Journaling: How Journal Writing Can Support a Life of Wellness, Creativity, Meaning and Purpose.*

In my role as a leader in the journal writing realm, I receive hundreds of questions about journaling and have discovered some of the key questions people have. This book is largely motivated by the desire to offer some answers to the types of questions below and share the wisdom of our inspiring contributors:

- What should I write about?
- How often should I journal?
- How can I write consistently and create the journaling habit?
- How can I go deeper with journaling?
- How can I get the most out of journaling?
- How can I keep my journaling fresh and interesting?
- How can I use journaling for specific purposes, such as:
  - › Improving my health
  - › Decreasing my stress
  - › Dealing with anxiety and depression
  - › Solving my problems
  - › Gaining clarity for life decisions
  - › Becoming more creative
  - › Feeling happier
  - › Making career choices
  - › Overcoming grief and loss

- ➤ Manifesting dreams and goals
- ➤ Increasing my self-awareness

In this book, we have brought together forty renowned journal writing enthusiasts and experts to share with you an abundance of journaling techniques. In the pages that follow, these journal writers offer an engaging array of journal writing prompts and activities to enliven and enrich your own personal journaling practice.

As for me, I have been a journal writer since I was a child. I love journal writing! My friends gift me beautiful journals. My teenage son recently spent $65 to buy me a designer journal and his thoughtful gift really touched my heart. I have never spent that much money on a journal in my entire life! My husband buys me colorful pens while teasing me that I have too many pens (and he might be right). I can spend hours in bookstores and stationary stores. Does this sound familiar?

I had no way of knowing that this personal hobby of simply writing down my thoughts and feelings and lists and doodles and poems and hopes and more could have, all these years later, become so central to who I have become and to the work I do in the world. Serendipity merged with passion and unleashed a dream somewhere in my heart to see manifest an organization that devoted itself to teaching about the healing and transformational power of writing.

In fact, it was my personal journaling, in great measure, that led to me discovering my desire to teach. This epiphany led me to start a business called Creative Wellness, where I spent years developing and teaching writing for self-care, resilience, and wellness programs focused on burnout prevention for helping and healthcare professionals.

I might not have done this without the idea for Creative Wellness emerging many times in the pages of my journal. From this awareness came action, and I embarked on an entrepreneurial path aligned with my passions for self-care and wellness through writing. This work led me to learn of an organization called the International Association for Journal Writing (IAJW.org), founded by Ruth Folit. I became a member of the IAJW and then offered an online course. I've always deeply valued the mission of this organization.

Ruth invited me to carry on the work of the IAJW as her successor and in 2018, I became the Director of the International Association for Journal Writing. I am honored to grow and lead a global community of journal writers, as well as offer a suite of online journaling courses, tools, e-books, and virtual events including writing circles, retreats, and workshops. There is not a week that goes by that I am not writing, speaking, or teaching about the many benefits of, and creative approaches to, journal writing.

I believe that journal writing is fundamentally a journey to self. It is a journey that influences the whole of our lives. You will see many versions of this same type of journey with journaling in the pages of this book— where journaling leads people to life changes, leaps of faith, new insights, and meaningful decisions. Journal writing can help you gain clarity and discover your life purposes and passions. It can also support you to cultivate the courage and self-trust you need to take action on all of your dreams and desires that emerge on the page.

My greatest hope for you as you read this book is that you are inspired to write for yourself and to take your personal writing to the next level, whatever that might mean to you. Perhaps you want to start journaling, keep journaling, or return to it, if you have forsaken it along the way.

Now, open *The Great Book of Journaling*. There is so much inspiration here. Embrace where your writing takes you! And while you are writing, know that there are journal writers all around the world also moving pen over paper.

CHAPTER 1

Juicy Journaling

By SARK

"I hope you will go out and let stories, that is life, happen to you, and that you will work with these stories from your life—not someone else's life—water them with your blood and tears and your laughter till they bloom, till you yourself burst into bloom. That is the work. The only work."

—Clarissa Pinkola Estes

Welcome to your curious, friendly, inspired writer self! Welcome also to your resistant, crabby, or avoiding parts that might feel afraid to write anything.

Juicy Journaling contains *all* the parts of you—not just the easiest or most attractive parts.

I've been practicing what I call Juicy Journaling for forty-two years, and it's a place for me to:

- Feel myself as I am at any moment
- Be and become more of who I actually am
- Practice compassionately witnessing my experiences and feelings
- Heal from horrifying and more ordinary traumas
- Play with new insights and awareness
- Invent over what doesn't feel juicy
- Explore new kinds of consciousnesses

- Record my dreams
- Share my life as I'm living it
- Reflect on what has happened or rehearse the future
- Process memories
- Surprise myself
- Understand how I operate in the world
- Investigate my resistances
- Make declarations and intentions
- Confess things I don't understand
- Name things I might not be able to say out loud
- Create and write the new while living it
- Celebrate and name miraculous moments and experiences
- Detail everything I'm glad about

Juicy Journaling has led me to:

- Publish eighteen bestselling books and travel the world, meeting my readers and writing along my way
- Create a successful lifestyle brand and business
- Speak and teach about the infinite power of creativity in action
- Live my purpose as a transformer, uplifter, and laser beam of love, and offer that through my art, words, and spirit
- Publish a soulful weekly Magic Blog
- Magically Mentor other writers and creators to begin, continue, or complete books and other creative projects
- Create and teach innovative writing programs

Here are some of my recommendations for writing:

- Write now and keep writing
- If your writing bores you, let it lead you somewhere else
- Let yourself be originally you with your writing
- Invest in juicy pens and thirsty paper
- Release old stories you habitually tell and write new ones
- Forgive yourself for every word you haven't written
- Dare to quit your writing and start over
- Free your thinking and let new words form

- Honor your tender, scared parts while you write
- Allow your genius to be seen and known

One of my very favorite recommendations is to write your life as you live it. Write your stories. The ones that only *you* can tell.

A powerful way to write more is to use my MicroMOVEment Miracle Method. This is what I created almost thirty years ago to write what I dreamed of while still sometimes procrastinating, avoiding, and resisting writing.

This works because starting smaller will cause you to start more often instead of just thinking about what you want to start writing!

I also use my MicroMOVEment Miracle Method to do everything in my life because it beautifully supports my writing between going to the dentist, doing taxes, napping, avoiding, fooling around, and all the rest of what we do as humans.

Quick Things to Know about MicroMOVEments

MicroMOVEments are like an ignition system. They are a way to get started with your writing. They are five minutes in length or even less. I designed this method to work in five-minute increments because I figured I could do just about anything for five minutes. Most people are high achievers or overachievers and will immediately question how "enough" writing can get done in five minutes. It works better than not starting at all or trying to do too much and getting crabby and tired.

My thirty years of research show that we'll keep going 60 percent of the time if we can just get started. For the 40 percent of the time that you don't keep going, using MicroMOVEments convinces the brain that something is happening with your writing, and this part of the brain doesn't care if it's five minutes or five hours of work—it stops you from constantly knowing that you're not doing anything with your writing. This is powerFULL and will create great internal shifts that will change your writing habits forever.

MicroMOVEments help you to stop using your mind as a filing cabinet and gives your writing plans a physical home and plan.

MicroMOVEments cause a "habit of completion," which circumvents a habit of procrastination.

The MicroMOVEment Miracle Method is customizable to your style, and results will expand the more you make this method "yours."

Creating Your Center and Choosing MicroMOVEments

The main way to create what you want with your writing is to create the "center description." This means that you'll be writing down what you desire for your writing in a way that pleases or delights you. What you write in the center wants to be delightful.

I've become aware that we do and create the most when we're delighted, inspired, moved, amused, and feeling good with our writing and writing processes.

Examples of MicroMOVEment Centers

You *write* what you desire in the center. You can write in the center of a piece of paper.

Here are two examples:

- Create and complete my super inspiring novel
- Easily and joyfully publish my book

The way we describe our desires becomes what happens to them!

Create MicroMOVEments to Bring Your Center to Life

I recommend adding delight or amusement to your MicroMOVEments because when you add delight, you'll use them even more! Write a tiny movement on the paper you wrote your center on or use a Post-It.

Examples of delightFULL MicroMOVEments

- Play an *amazing* title game for my novel.
- Take out a shoebox of index cards with writing ideas and fling them into the air. Wherever the cards land, start writing from that point.

The main point is to create easy movement; *any* movement will lead to more movement. You can think of the MicroMOVEment Miracle Method as yoga for your mind. Tiny movements will lead to huge results.

Develop a "micro mindset" where you realize that continuing is the *whole* point and that your writing *process* is equal in value to the results you seek. Think tinier, smaller, much smaller, then tinier and tinier still. This will result in words getting written.

It's so much more *fun* to have an easy way to make more writing miracles and creative magic in our lives. A micro mindset does that most of all! Make it smaller, and you'll start more often and become a *happy finisher* of writing rather than someone who rarely starts.

Also, pay less attention to creating the MicroMOVEments than you do to actually moving. If you find one or more MicroMOVEments that work, keep using them. I've used one for years that keeps working:

Find my lucky purple pen and put it next to the chaise lounge.

This led to at least a dozen books being written and published.

I micromove daily with my writing, and I exuberantly recommend it.

· · · · · · · · · · · · · · ·

Here's some of what I don't recommend about writing:

- Resisting writing—it's harder than actually writing
- Performing in your journal
- Writing what you think people will want to read
- Feeling like all your writing needs to be "good"
- Holding back from writing excruciatingly embarrassing things
- Not exploring all your challenging emotions
- Complaining about how much you're not writing
- Judging what you write and finding it lacking before doing the work of crafting it to say what you want

- Quitting or not continuing before you've written what only you can write

Here are some ways to play and practice Juicy Journaling with prompts:

- What I didn't say out loud today...
- Something unexpectedly beautiful was...
- How I fell in love with a new part of myself today...
- The crabbiest part of today was...
- The miracle of today...
- Today's wildest dream...
- The quietest part inside me today...
- Right now, *write* whatever is in your heart.
- Start: "Right now, I'm wondering about _____"
  and see where that leads you.

Go deeper, say more, and write about all the *other* thoughts and feelings—the ones that surprise you, scare you, delight you, or embarrass you. Allow yourself to write words that are quintessentially *real*. Describe the places inside you that jump for joy or collapse in fear.

How can you care exquisitely for yourself with all your emotions? What brings out your best, most magic self?

Instead of saying "on a lighter note," say "on a darker note," and see what comes. What does it mean to live your life in full color? What color(s) most represents your life right now, and why? What color(s) would you *like* to represent your life right now, and why?

What is the juiciest thing imaginable that you would dare to write about? Go ahead... write it, write now! Let your writing be juicy!

Create a fast list of your favorite gorgeous moments, such as the smell of clothes dried in the sun. List two to twenty-five gorgeous moments as quickly as you think of them. Add details like "perfectly steamed broccoli glowing in the pan." I think that fast lists are a great way to get writing moving. When your writing is moving, it can make miracles.

Give yourself permission to allow the fun of flow in your writing. Your writing will respond beautifully to you letting it flow.

Flowing is nonlinear; it's full of grace and wonder. Fresh glistening peaches and slants of sunlight are commonly seen during times of flow. Flowing can occur in the bathtub and the shower. Notice that water *flows*, as your writing will when you allow it. The state of flow loves surprises and new environments.

Take yourself and your writing somewhere brand new and *fun*! Let your stories tumble out. You have treasure chests of stories inside that are of great value. Let them out so that others may benefit from them. Hoard nothing. And do not wait for the inner perfectionist to approve, or you will wait a lifetime.

I also invite you to rest and reset with your writing. It's natural at the start of writing something to feel energized, hopeful, and optimistic. It's also natural to start enthusiastically and then experience living life as an interruption to one's writing life.

I support you in seeing and feeling your value as a writer, whether you are writing or not.

If you wish to publish, let your full heart lead your journey. When we focus on the song of our soul and heart, then others will be touched similarly.

Sometimes people wonder or worry whether people will like or approve of their creative expression. It's none of your business. It's your business to stay present and focused on the work of your deepest dreams. It might look crooked, strange, or odd, but if it delights you, it is yours and will find its way into other hearts.

All your creative dreams and writing will grow if you help make them *real* and let them bloom.

The time is truly now, and your stories and wonderful words are needed. We need your creative spirit in action because there is only one of you.

Your words and stories need a human channel to bring them down to earth, and that human channel is you!

Love,
SARK

About the Author

SARK (Susan Ariel Rainbow Kennedy) is a bestselling author, artist, inspirationalist, and acclaimed teacher and mentor. Her purpose in life is to be an uplifter, transformer, and laser beam of love—she offers that with love through her art, words, and spirit. To learn more about SARK, visit **PlanetSARK.com**

CHAPTER 2

Journaling Basics

By Mari L. McCarthy

*"Journaling is like whispering to one's self
and listening at the same time."*

—Mina Murray

Your Journaling Journey

Writing in your journal is simultaneously simple and profound. There is nothing complicated about putting pen to paper, but when you make it a regular habit, it becomes a powerful force for good in your life.

In your journal, you uncover your innermost thoughts, feelings, desires, and fears. You release stress, spark creativity, and overcome challenges. You gain insights that lead to growth, adventure, and change. You heal old wounds and cultivate healthier relationships with yourself and others. It's one of the most affordable and effective ways you can care for yourself.

Journaling is truly transformative; it is shown to improve physical, mental, and emotional health and help you achieve your goals. But even if you understand all the benefits, you might still struggle with building a journaling practice.

How to Overcome Common Journaling Challenges

Do any of these obstacles sound familiar?

- I can't seem to find the time to write
- I used to journal but stopped when life got busy
- I don't know what to write about
- I have too much I want to write about
- I like the idea of journaling but not the actual practice
- I feel bored/restless/anxious/overwhelmed when I write
- I forget to journal (and then feel bad about it)

If you recognize yourself in one or more of these statements, you are in good company! These are common challenges that afflict even the most dedicated journal writers.

The good news is that you can use one simple guideline to help you overcome them all: *Write a little bit every day.*

That's it. Strive for consistency, not perfection. Some days you may write pages and pages without stopping; other days, you may manage only a sentence. Either way is fine. Simply aim to write something in your journal every single day. If you miss one day, don't beat yourself up about it; just start again the next day with fresh energy.

After a while, you won't even have to think about it. Journaling will become an integral part of your day that you do automatically, like brushing your teeth or drinking your coffee every morning. Over time, you will start to see the positive changes journaling is making in your life—giving you a safe place to blow off steam, process emotions, explore ideas, or set goals.

Treat journaling like any other habit you value. You wouldn't go for a jog, do yoga, or practice the piano once a year and expect to see huge progress. But if you set aside a few minutes every day to run, stretch, or play, you would soon notice the difference and reap the benefits of your efforts. The same is true for journaling. The more often you write, the more benefits you will experience from your journaling practice.

My Journaling Story

I think of myself as an unlikely journaler. For decades, I have used my journaling practice to help me accomplish my personal and professional goals and create a happy, healthy, and fulfilling life. I have created a thriving community of journalers from around the world that brings me joy and inspiration every day.

But this wasn't always the case. Almost thirty years ago, I had what was supposed to be my dream job. I was a partner in a successful business consulting firm, working with Fortune 100 companies all over the country. I spent my days constantly on the go—flying from one meeting to the next, working into the wee hours of the morning, and packing my schedule full to bursting.

I rarely took the time to listen to what my body or my mind needed. Sleep? No time for that! Food, water, exercise, rest? Later! I was a serial overachiever, and I was proud of all that I was accomplishing. I pushed aside the signs of burnout—aching shoulders, severe headaches, mounting exhaustion—until one day, I couldn't ignore these stress symptoms any longer.

I began to notice that something was off with my coordination. I started losing my balance frequently. I ran into walls. I had strange sensations in my legs and arms. At first, I chalked it up to stress and kept trying to power through and maintain my usual schedule. After increasingly serious symptoms and a series of doctor visits, I was diagnosed with multiple sclerosis (MS), a chronic and degenerative disease that affects the brain and spinal cord.

Until that point, I had been treating my body like a machine that existed only to support my fast-paced lifestyle. I thought with my brain only, not recognizing the interconnectedness of my physical, mental and emotional health.

My diagnosis was a profound turning point for me. I had to admit that my whole self needed to be loved and cared for—mind, body, and spirit—and journaling became the way I reconnected my inner and outer life. I learned to tune into my health by beginning to journal every morning without fail, even teaching myself to write with my left, nondominant hand out of necessity. My penmanship grew steadier over time, and so did the thoughts that poured out of me.

I told myself: *Just write. Anything that comes to mind.* It wasn't always easy, but I kept at it every day. I stopped ignoring my pesky feelings and physical symptoms. Instead, I got curious and started asking questions. When something was bothering me, I'd dig deeper and ask: *What's going on here?*

As I continued my daily writing practice, my MS symptoms improved. More importantly, I slowly got back in touch with my whole, true self. Journaling has transformed every aspect of my life: helping me make healthy lifestyle changes, find harmony between my mind and body, start my own business, uncover my creative talents, and rewrite unhelpful old messaging.

I know I can't control everything that happens to me, but I *can* deal with whatever comes my way.

Try This

Here are some tips for starting your journaling practice and making it an essential part of your life.

Connect with Your "Why"

Ask yourself why you are drawn to journaling. What sparked your interest in it? How does it tie into your identity or your goals? How do you hope it will help you gain insights or make positive changes?

Start Small

Every sentence counts! Remember that your objective is just to write a little bit every day. If you're intimidated by the blank page, set a daily journaling goal you are sure to meet. Commit to writing a single sentence or write for one minute. You can always do more if you want to and scale up as you get more comfortable. But set the bar low at first so you guarantee your success, and then celebrate your small win.

Pair Journaling with an Existing Habit

Journaling becomes an effortless habit when you do it at the same time every day. Think about when would make the most sense for your schedule and preferences. Is there a daily habit you could combine with journaling?

If you're a morning person, you could add a few minutes of journaling with your breakfast and tea before work. If you like to take a midday break, you could journal when you get back from your usual walk. If you have a nightly reading ritual, you could write before opening your book.

Experiment to Find Your Style

There's no right or wrong way to journal, and what you enjoy may evolve over time. Have fun with it and play with different styles, prompts, and activities. For example:

- **Gratitude:** Jot down a few things you're grateful for each day and how they make you feel.
- **Daydreaming:** Play the "what if" game and let your imagination run wild. What big dreams do you have? What ideas light you up? What would your ideal job, partner, home, life look like?
- **Mental decluttering:** Get all those jumbled thoughts out of your head and onto the page. Do one to three pages of stream-of-consciousness writing.
- **Q&A:** Have a conversation with your journal, asking it any questions that come up (and offering answers if you have them!). Explore a problem you're grappling with or try to figure out how you feel about something. Lead with curiosity and compassion. When in doubt, ask: *What's going on here?*

- **Self-compassion:** Share something that is bothering you, then write a response as if you are talking to a close friend. Be empathetic, kind, and loving, and tell yourself what you need to hear.

Creating a journaling practice is a long-term investment in your health and happiness—and one of the most rewarding habits you can build. Good luck in the next steps of your journaling journey.

About the Author

Mari L. McCarthy is the founder and Chief Empowerment Officer of CreateWriteNow, where she provides ideas, inspiration, and therapeutic journaling resources for health-conscious people who want to heal their issues and express their true selves. She is the award-winning author of *Journaling Power: How To Create The Happy, Healthy Life You Want To Live* and *Heal Your Self With Journaling Power* and the creator of over twenty *Journaling Power* workbooks.

CHAPTER 3

Journaling Simplicity

By Kathleen Adams

"Writing a journal is like having a box of magic wands."

—A client

I remember with fondness the long, languid journal writing sessions of my youth—a halcyon time before cell phones, email, faxes, even answering machines. I typically wrote for two uninterrupted hours each day, spilling my dramas, recording my dreams, and analyzing my thoughts and feelings. I have dozens of boxes in storage, stuffed with wide-lined spiral notebooks from those years, meticulous chronicles of my twenties and thirties.

By my forties, life was more complex. My private practice in journal therapy was growing roots and buds, the internet was a shiny new toy, and my routine two-hour journal sessions were a distant memory.

My journal was still an active part of my lifestyle, but my schedule begged for something more pragmatic. I discovered the power of "small and simple" in my counseling practice. Nearly all my clients were willing to use writing as a tool in our work together. But I found that most of my clients echoed my own circumstances: "I'm so busy! Work is so stressful! Kids are so demanding! I don't have time to write!"

The answer? Journal simplicity!

What Is Journal Simplicity?

Journal simplicity is about keeping it short, savory, and simple without sacrificing insight or effectiveness.

- **Short:** Five minutes or less.
- **Savory:** Juicy and rich.
- **Simple:** Easy, sensible structures.

Journal simplicity is the center of a Venn diagram in which short writing techniques, savory writing prompts, and simple writing practices are equal circles.

Short Writing Techniques

Starting with my first Journal to the Self (then, Write On!) workshop in 1985, my primary theory about journal therapy has been that there are many ways to write, and each way has individual benefits. I call these ways "techniques." My early years developed my theories about how each technique, its own unique wand in the box, worked its magic. Some techniques are imbued with the magic of packing a big punch of clarity and insight in two to seven minutes.

Savory Writing Prompts

With super-short techniques we rely on savory writing prompts to stimulate juicy questions or below-the-surface thoughts or ideas.

Simple Writing Practices

The therapeutic writing world has standard writing practices that have become conventions. Journal simplicity adds practices that are particularly helpful for short, savory, and simple writing.

Three Short Techniques

1. **The Five-Minute Sprint.** This is exactly what it sounds like: Set a timer for five minutes and blast away. You can do it spontaneously when you're mad, sad, or scared, or you can write to a savory prompt.

Whatever you do, write fast and furious and don't stop to think. Unless your writing takes an interesting turn on its own, try to stay on topic. When the timer rings, finish your thought, read it back, and write a reflection, the instructions for which will follow.

Two things make the Five-Minute Sprint especially useful. One is that nearly everyone agrees five minutes is an accessible unit of time. The second is that when you know you only have five minutes, the bottom line rises to meet you. You get more done in less time, usually with robust outcomes. Paired with the reflection write, you may discover surprising insight, clarity, and action orientation.

2. **Captured Moments.** Just as a camera captures a moment in time on film (or in pixels), the journal Captured Moment freezes an experience of emotional intensity in prose. One of the hallmarks is how it is written from the five senses—sight, sound, smell, taste, touch—and then brings in the sixth sense of emotional connection. Use juicy verbs and extravagant adjectives to help capture intensity. Writing in the present tense, as if you are back in that original moment, gives immediacy to your storytelling and may make it easier to enter the experience fully.

   Although the technique of Captured Moments is not biased toward positive experiences, I tend to recommend it for capturing highs rather than lows. Many people are naturally fluent in writing about difficulties, pain, loss, and challenge. They are less practiced at writing about life's small pleasures, the ones that brighten a day or lift a mood or give a deep "ahhhh" of peace. Captured Moments of beauty, intimacy, grace, connection, or generosity help us remember that within the sea of challenges are reliable islands of safety and comfort.

3. **Reflection Write.** The reflection write offers immediate feedback on your process and brings clarity and insight that might otherwise

go unharvested. It is often the most important two minutes of any writing process.

Because the journal, by its nature, is a present-tense document, you might turn the page and go on to the next moment without savoring the wisdom of your own words. This is unfortunate; there is insight to be harvested in just about every story.

The reflection write begins with a read-back of what has been written, followed by a sentence or two of feedback: *As I read this, I notice....* Or, *I am surprised by...* Or, *I suddenly see....* Or anything similar. Stay open for insights and clarity.

Three Simple Practices

There is a set of conventions collectively agreed to be useful for satisfying journal writing: Write quickly, write honestly, date your entries, protect your privacy, stop writing if it starts feeling unmanageable, keep what you write or destroy it with intention, and let your Authentic Self take center stage. Each of these practices applies to journal simplicity. Here are three more that are specific to writing small and simple.

1. **Practice time integrity.** The power of a Five-Minute Sprint depletes rapidly when it cannot reliably be contained to five minutes. If you want to write longer when the timer chimes, make a conscious renegotiation of your time and attention. Don't get lazy with time boundaries. If you find that five minutes simply isn't enough, then write Ten-Minute Sprints.

2. **Three feeling words.** If you are skeptical that anything useful can happen in a five-minute writing period, try this simple reality check. At the start of an entry, write three words or phrases that describe how you feel. Then write. At the end, read back and reflect. Then write three words or phrases that describe how you feel. Compare the word sets. That's how your emotional state shifted in five minutes of writing. This

is an excellent practice for any write, especially highly emotionally charged ones, to document the real-time effects of writing.

Sometimes there won't be much difference, and occasionally you could feel worse at the end than at the beginning. Most of the time, though, it can be surprising to discover that you can go from *confused, down, stressed* to *energized, clear, determined* in the space of five minutes plus a reflection.

3. **Series of three.** Any write that feels potent could benefit from the "series of three" approach, which is to zoom in on one interesting or provocative aspect and spin it into a follow-on write for a deeper dive. For instance, in the Try This section below is a prompt called Different and Better, followed by Getting Unstuck. These two can be written in sequence and followed by a third, perhaps Action Plan or Next Steps.

There are times when I need a long, luxurious journal write in the same way that my body craves protein or sunshine. In between, however, I'm grateful for the reliable magic of journaling simplicity!

Try This

Prompts: Five-Minute Sprint

Typically, you will start a Five-Minute Sprint with an uninterrupted seven-minute stretch of time (includes thirty seconds for entry and ninety seconds for reflection). Have a fresh screen or page and preferred writing utensil ready in advance. Set your phone or watch timer to five minutes. Write as quickly as is comfortable, pausing only to let the next thought bubble up. It's okay to scribble and make typos (don't fix them yet). When the timer rings, finish your sentence and read back. Write a sentence or two of reflection.

- **Different and Better.** Recall a situation, issue, project, relationship that is currently stressful or otherwise out of balance. Write to this question: *If I woke up tomorrow morning and things were resolved, what would be different and better?* Be specific. Reflect on what it would take to build the bridge from familiar and stressful to different and better.
- **Getting Unstuck.** Bring to mind an impasse, roadblock, logjam, rut—perhaps the current stressor you wrote about. Then brainstorm action steps you could take, starting right now, to move forward. Choose one and make a quick outline of what, when, and how you will proceed. Repeat until time is up. Then take action!
- **Three Little Words.** Choose any three-word slogan, maxim, phrase of inspiration, or advice and use it as the title of a Five-Minute Sprint. Write to that theme. Here are some starters.
    › *What's Going On?*—This present-centered Sprint helps you identify and articulate whatever is hiding in plain sight.
    › *Just Do It**—This registered trademark of Nike concisely tells a universal truth: The way out is through. What is your "it," and what can you "just do"?
    › *Up Until Now*—These three little words are powerful when you're transitioning from an old story (habit, behavior, lifestyle) to a new one. *Up until now, I've been... and starting now, I can be...*
    › *What Just Happened?*—This prompt is useful for sudden intrusions, blindsides, or surprises—times when your brain might go briefly offline. Telling a rapid, concise, cohesive story helps restore your capacity to think straight.

Prompts: Captured Moments

The Captured Moment is designed to be written from the senses. Try a closed-eye relaxation. Bring your topic to mind and immerse yourself in sensory memory. This is one of the more creative techniques, so reach for enlivened and descriptive language. Write quickly and revise later if you choose. Write for seven minutes and reflect after. Allow extra time for revision if you want to craft your piece.

- **Beauty.** Not everyone agrees on what is beautiful, but nearly everyone recognizes what they think of as beauty when they see or experience it. Beauty refreshes us and reaches places of peace and harmony where stress cannot coexist. Begin with attention and awareness. Find moments to capture: Stand on the porch and watch the sunrise. Arrange a perfect rose in a bud vase. Gaze into the curious eyes of a child.

- **Success.** Remember a time when you felt successful from the inside out. Recall the feeling, where you were, who you were with, and what was said or done. Write it in sensory detail, including the positive accolades you received and your proud self-talk. Imbedding memories of personal success helps awaken your mind and memory to the truth that you have a personal relationship with success that can be replicated.

- **Intimacy.** If you could transform your relationship with your partner or strengthen the bond of connection with a moody child in just five minutes, would you? Write a Captured Moment of a special time together—harmonious teamwork with your partner, belly-laughing with your kid, a moment of tenderness shared—and tuck it into a lunch sack or jeans pocket or under a pillow.

About the Author

Kathleen (Kay) Adams LPC, PTR, is a Colorado licensed therapist and registered journal/poetry therapist. She is the founder and director of the Center for Journal Therapy, Inc. and its two online schools: Therapeutic Writing Institute, a professional training credentials program, and the personal growth school, Journalversity. Kay is the author/editor of fourteen books in the field, including the classic *Journal to the Self* (1990) and her most recent duo, *Journal Therapy for Calming Anxiety* (2020) and *Journal Therapy for Overcoming Burnout* (2022).

CHAPTER 4

Journaling Resistance

By Liz Crocker

"It's easy after all not to be a writer. Most people are not writers, and very little harm comes to them."

—Julian Barnes

You may have begun this chapter because you read sequentially, and this is where you are. But maybe when you looked at the Table of Contents, you saw the word "resistance" and said, "That's the one for me."

First, a confession. I don't write in a journal, and, essentially, I never have. That's a slight exaggeration because, for a year or two as a teenager, I kept a locked diary, filling it with self-important gibberish. I have also kept travel notebooks when I've explored different places in the world.

Over the years, many friends have earnestly extolled the virtues of journaling, but I've always been ready with various reasons why I don't journal. However, even as defensive justifications have come out of my mouth, voices in my head simultaneously presented counterarguments. Welcome to my internal debate!

Typical Reasons Not to Keep a Journal...
Along With Rebuttals

Reason 1: "I don't have time."

Rebuttal: You are saying you don't want to commit to taking time to sit down and write about your thoughts and feelings. It's not that your head is empty—in fact, it's likely there's always chatter in your head as you have a shower, walk, take the bus, drive your car. Might you want to capture any of that? Could you possibly sort out that complex problem if you jotted down pros and cons? Journaling doesn't have to be about the activities of your life—its value rests more with the process of embracing and reflecting on the patterns of thought and emotions that are constantly looping around within you.

Reason 2: "I have beautiful journals waiting for me, but I don't want to ruin them. For example, a slim, lime green one with pages of faint graph paper teases me with its gold-lettered question on the cover— 'What kind of human do you wanna be?' What if I start to answer that question and say nothing interesting or make a spelling mistake or use a blotchy pen?"

Rebuttal: Stop fussing over what to write in. It's just a journal and will be wasted if it lies empty. If you fear your words won't be worthy, use scraps of paper as drafts to transcribe later or write on sticky notes and place them on a wall or inside your still-perfect journal on those beautiful graph paper pages. And spelling mistakes? Well, one of the advantages of writing just for yourself is not having to care about spelling!

Reason 3: "If I tell my truth on paper, especially about what I think or feel about others, I'm afraid my words will be found. I would hate for my writing to be read by others and be misunderstood, possibly causing pain."

Rebuttal: If you are worried about your writing being discovered, find a brilliant hiding place that is still easy for you to access. Also, make a pact with a trusted friend who promises to find and destroy your journals if something happens to you. Alternatively, you could pretend you are a spy and write in a code only you understand. And you can always throw out what you write. Whoever said you have to keep what you've written? Isaac Asimov said, "The writer's best friend is the wastepaper basket." Frankly, journal writing is more about the process than it is about the creation of a Pulitzer.

Reason 4: "I have other ways of remembering people/places/events. I already have artifacts from my past that spark memories: old datebooks; photo albums; friends' handwritten, food-stained recipe cards; birthday cards and letters to Santa; an old-chipped bowl from a favorite aunt; stuffed animals from childhood; postcards from places visited; children's report cards and early drawings; my husband's wedding band and his favorite shirt."
Rebuttal: Great! You've got scads of material prompts, so why not write about that old bowl or your favorite aunt or why you've kept what you have? Allow evocative words to come to the surface and see what emotions the words bring with them. Savor what is evoked, and then share these descriptions about what you have kept and why so that others might know. Louise de Salvo commented that "journaling, if it is shared, can be an act of generosity."

Reason 5: "I'm not very disciplined, and I don't tend to do the things I 'should.'"
Rebuttal: That may be true, but it doesn't let you off the hook for occasionally trying. Something is better than nothing. And maybe you can consider replacing "should" with "want." Figure out what might be in it for you.

Now for a second confession. In spite of myself, I know expressive writing and journaling can be deeply beneficial. Wiser people than I have given testimony to the power of writing. For example, Horace Walpole explained, "I never understand anything until I have written about it."

I first learned about the benefits of writing, even if it's only occasional or situational, through being in a writing group. We used a technique called "spontaneous writing"—picking a random word and just writing, without forethought, for ten minutes.

Time and time again, through these ten-minute writing experiences, I discovered memories and emotions that I didn't even know were buried within or had "eureka moments" when I suddenly learned something new about myself. For example, when writing *Transforming Memories* with two other women and reflecting on the impacts of having had an alcoholic parent, this bubbled up from within and out onto the page:

> *Why do I cry? I have observed that I typically cry in response to stories of exquisite kindness and tender love or to recalling profound moments of loving and being loved or to witnessing expressions of a deep sadness from the lack of love or love lost. I recently had a possible epiphany which is this: it occurs to me that the reason I am so touched by these "love moments" is that I had a big hole to fill up, the hole created in childhood from not believing I was enough or worthy of love. Recognizing this is helping me to receive love graciously, with both gratitude and delight, and to offer it purely, not because I want to change someone.*

Even though I still resist the idea of keeping a journal, I do often use short bursts of writing as a safe way to, as Fritz Perls, a German-born psychiatrist, once said, "lose your mind and come to your senses." If I'm wrestling with a weighty problem, I have learned that simply jotting down key words and salient points can tame the hurricane in my head, with its swirling dark clouds, bolts of lightning, jarring reverberations of thunder, and destabilizing winds. Transferring such internal chaos and angst from my heart and head to neutral paper can guide me to the typical calm and clear sky when a storm ends.

I used writing in this way recently when, one day, spontaneous tears started to run down my face. I knew I was stressed, and my heart was feeling heavy about a situation over which I had no control. I was riddled with concern but feeling powerless. A voice inside me said, "Get it out." I grabbed a notebook and a pen and hurriedly scribbled words, phrases, and frustrations until I calmed down enough to go for a walk. Amazingly, when I returned from the wonders of fresh air and nature, I felt better and decided to rip up what I'd written as a way of literally and figuratively "letting it all go." My fretful and explosive writing had worked its magic.

Now It's Your Turn—Try This

1. **Look for, collect, and reflect on quotes.** When one speaks to you, write it down, and then let your own words come. Here are some to start with:
   - A section from the poem *Ulysses* by Alfred Lord Tennyson:
     > "I am a part of all that I have met
     > Yet all experience is an arch wherethro'
     > Gleams the untraveled world
     > Whose margin fades
     > Forever and ever when I move."
   - Who have you met; who influenced or affected you? When, where, and how?
     > "There's a crack in everything. That's how the light gets in."
     > —Leonard Cohen
   - Have you had moments of darkness? Did a crack appear to let the light in?
     > "We can't return to our childhood and ask that it be different. We need to learn how to accept, nurture, and fulfill ourselves."
     > —Tara Brach
   - What did you like best and least about your childhood? What do you do to nurture and fulfill yourself?

2. **Create some provocative questions for yourself and answer them in ten minutes:**
   - Who's the most interesting stranger you have ever met?
   - What's your favorite book/song?
   - Where would you go with a free plane ticket and why there?
   - Are you a "glass-half-full" or a "glass-half-empty" person?
   - Would you prefer to be a giraffe or a three-toed sloth or a...?
3. **Consider the day.** If blank pages are unsettling, try some of these reflective prompts:
   - It is said that curiosity and judgment cannot occupy the same space at the same time. Which hat did you wear today—the curious or judgmental one?
   - Consider this maxim: "We nourish from overflow, not emptiness." Did your day nourish or empty you, or both? How?
   - Anne Lamott wrote a book titled *Help! Thanks! Wow! The Three Essential Prayers.* Did you ask for help today? Did you show/ speak your gratitude to someone? Did you feel inspired and, if so, by what?

Julian Barnes noted that little harm comes to writers, and so, even if you feel reluctant, consider dipping your toes in the water of words. You may be astonished and delighted to see where the current takes you.

About the Author

Liz Crocker is the co-author of *Privileged Presence: Personal Stories of Connections in Health Care* and *Transforming Memories: Sharing Spontaneous Writing Using Loaded Words.* In addition to being a writer and an editor, Liz has been a teacher, entrepreneur, health consultant, and policy advisor. She founded and still proudly owns Canada's oldest children's bookstore (Woozles) and openly admits to being obsessively passionate about reading and sharing books.

CHAPTER 5

The Reflective Journal

By Lynda Monk

"Reflective practice invites you to rediscover your creative potential, and to find more ways to be nourished by what you do in work and in life."

—Marlena Field & Donna Martin, authors of *Simply Being: A Reflective Practice Guide for Helping Professionals*

People often use journaling for two key purposes: to document the happenings in their days and lives, and to vent thoughts and feelings. Both are legitimate ways to journal. I would like to suggest that there is also a deeper and more intentional way to journal that can bring about a wide range of additional benefits than simply writing about the events of your day or venting feelings. This is what I refer to as the reflective journaling method.

Regular self-reflection and the act of reflecting on life in meaningful ways are important practices that can help us become wiser and more compassionate with ourselves and others. Reflection can also lead to greater self-awareness, understanding and acceptance, qualities, and ways of being that can support us in everything we do.

Reflective journaling can be transformational. Why? Because it involves asking questions of yourself and your life as a routine part of your journaling practice.

During my education to become a social worker and then years later during my coach certification program, I learned the transformational and healing power of good questions. As a helping professional, I was taught to listen deeply and ask purposeful questions, not so much to get the answer for myself as the listener but to help clients gain the answers from within for themselves.

Powerful questions are the cornerstone to curiosity, which is foundational to any type of learning and growth, including about oneself. The biggest question we might ask is the existential one, "Who am I?" We might write down and answer other questions like "What do I desire?" or "What do I need right now?" and "How can I meet that need?"

I once read that Einstein was quoted as saying that if he had one hour to solve a complex problem, he would spend the first fifty-five minutes coming up with a good question. Why? Because good questions lead to helpful, informative, and possibly even enlightening or life-changing answers.

When journaling, we want to write with an open mind, an open heart, and a willingness to learn new things about ourselves that we don't already know. In this way, the reflective journal is more than a regurgitation or simple documentation of the events of our lives; it is a powerful personal practice for greater self-discovery, increased self-awareness, and self-actualization. We can become the witness, the nonjudgmental observer, and the author of our own lives with the help of reflective journaling.

Reflective Journaling for Awareness-to-Action

Reflective journaling can also help us cross the bridge from increased self-awareness to taking action. For example, you can journal for a period of time, then pause and ask yourself, "So what and now what?" Or you can pause during your writing and ask: "What do I notice about what I wrote?"

This practice can help you integrate the new awareness you might be gaining as you journal with actions you want to take in your life. This makes journaling a reflective and action-oriented practice that can bring awakening, clarity, joy, and any desired changes into your life.

Here is an example from the pages of my journal where I engage in this awareness-to-action reflection:

January 11, 2021

These Covid times feel so heavy, like everything is on hold and stuck. Like nothing is moving or flowing like it used to, not even me. I need to keep moving my body—to walk in the forest, walk beside the ocean, with my sweet Sadie girl, my boys, my husband—connecting with the earth, my moving body, and the people I love all at once.

I need to trust that as I move, circumstances move too. As I breathe, the earth breathes. As I pause and listen within, I hear something greater than myself.

What do I notice about what I wrote? I notice that movement matters to me and it needs to be a daily priority in my life at this time.

Introducing Life Source Writing: A 5-Step Reflective Journaling Method

Several years ago, I created Life Source Writing, a five-step reflective journaling method for self-care, self-discovery, creativity, and wellness. I was in a yoga class, and at the end, when lying still in savasana (corpse pose or final resting place), I heard these words: "life source writing." I wondered what that meant! I did what any journal writer might do; I came home after the yoga class and wrote down these words in my journal: "What is life source writing?"

Five elements or steps emerged that could serve as a pathway to a holistic and reflective journaling method.

Life Source Writing is not a prescriptive five-step method but rather a holistic process that invites your mind, body, heart, and spirit into your journaling practice. You can consider this reflective method a road map to give each of your writing journeys or journaling times a meaningful beginning, a deeper middle, and an affirming completion infused with gratitude. This reflective journaling approach can ultimately support you to deepen your journaling practice and magnify the life-enriching benefits you can gain.

Life Source Writing is a process for using relaxed, spontaneous writing as a practice for self-awareness and personal well-being. Its five-step method integrates the natural healing properties of expressive writing with mindfulness, relaxation, inquiry, and affirmation to deepen your journaling while supporting you as the writer.

The 5 Steps of Life Source Writing

Step 1: Arrive (Mindfulness)

Arrive fully to the present moment and your writing. Mindful presence in the here and now is fuel for both your creative self-expression and well-being. You can simply acknowledge to yourself, "I am here now to write." You can also set an intention for your journaling, for example, "I would like to gain clarity about my true priorities while I write today." As Deepak Chopra said years ago when I heard him speak at a conference, "Attention energizes, intention transforms."

Step 2: Relax (Mind/Body Connection)

Take a moment to connect with your breath before writing. Breath is the energy of life moving through you, and it can support you to access your creative power. Breathe with awareness; even just a couple of slow, intentional breaths can help engage the relaxation response before you write. When we are relaxed, we can tap into our creativity and authentic voice on the page. Or, as Laraine Herring, author of *Writing Begins with the Breath: Embodying Your Authentic Voice*, puts it: "Returning to the rise and fall of the breath, bringing a level of conscious awareness to a predominantly involuntary action, reigns in the scatter nature of our thoughts and grounds us in our bodies, squarely in the present moment where we must remain if we are to write deeply."

Step 3: Write (Expressive Writing)

You have arrived fully to your writing; perhaps you have set a journaling intention, you are relaxed and have connected with your breath, your life source energy. This might have taken you a couple of minutes or longer. Now it is time to write. Simply go to the page and start writing. You might do a timed free-writing or use a journaling prompt or guided exercise to get you started. Remember, you are writing for yourself. Do not censor your writing, nor worry about grammar; simply write without judgment whatever wants to be written or expressed.

Step 4: Reflect (Inquiry, Feedback Loop)

After journaling, before stopping your writing time, you can pause and use further reflective prompts such as, "What I notice about what I wrote is…" or "What I feel about what I wrote is…" or "I can sense that…" or "I now realize…" etc. It is often our curiosity or questions that bring us to the page in the first place. This reflective step wrapped around the other side of your writing can help you gain more insights, healing, and growth from your journaling practice.

Step 5: Affirm (Gratitude Practice)

Bringing completion to your journal writing time in a brief yet purposeful way can bring a sense of closure and positivity to your writing. You might say or think something quietly to yourself, such as, "I am grateful for this time to reflect and write." Bringing our gratitude to anything, including our journaling, anchors us into a positive and uplifting emotional state. It is the perfect way to end your journaling time and transition from your reflective time on the page out into the rest of your day or night.

Conclusion

I have made many life decisions and changes based on insights and instincts that first appeared in the pages of my journal. Through engaging in deeper reflection with what flowed in my writing, new insights emerged. I have also grown to trust myself and my decisions with the help of my lifelong journaling practice. I have grown to appreciate that when certain thoughts and feelings repeatedly appear in my writing, a call to action is likely trying to get my attention.

For example, I have made the following decisions, to a great extent, because of the reflections and persistent instincts that appeared in my journal:

- To leave my first marriage
- To quit my career job as a medical social worker to start my own business
- To move to an island, at the age of thirty, where I had no job and didn't know a soul
- To trust that I could have children even when specialists told me there was a low probability that I could do so (I have two teenage sons)
- To get married again*

*Excerpt from My Journal, June 14, 2003:

I just came back from a walk. I am not sure what is happening. I started thinking about what it would be like to marry Peter. But why am I even thinking about this, I am never getting married again! I was clear with him about that early on in our relationship. I have been clear about this inside of myself for a few years now. What is going on? What is happening?

I continued to journal. Then something emerged on the page that brought me to tears and changed everything...

Why don't I want to get married again? What is this really all about?
Yes, I was devastated when Paul and I ended our marriage, and
that pain locked into me a solid decision that I never wanted to get
married again. But perhaps, it is not that I don't want to get married
again, maybe I never want to get divorced again?

Right there, in that moment, I knew something had changed. The insight that it was divorce I never wanted to experience again, not marriage itself, changed everything instantly. It allowed me to open to the possibility of marrying again. I sat with this insight that revealed itself through the writing itself and eventually I thought, *How can I act on this change? How can I let Peter know I've changed my mind about marriage?* While writing in my journal and reflecting on this, a new idea emerged: *I could ask him to marry me!*

On July 20, 2003, on Peter's forty-sixth birthday, at a Hawaiian luau-style birthday party with seventy of our friends present at our home, I gathered everyone's attention to make a toast for Peter and at the end, I asked him to marry me. He was shocked! And, he said yes.

I don't know if this clarity would have emerged if it were not for my reflective journaling practice. I was willing to ask myself questions on the page, then allow the answers to come, and then allow myself to act on that awareness.

Try This

Engage the five steps of Life Source Writing during one of your upcoming journaling times:

1. **Arrive.** Arrive fully to your writing time and perhaps set an intention for your journaling.
2. **Relax.** Breathe with awareness and invite your mind and body to relax.
3. **Write.** Write freely for a period of time and give yourself full permission to write whatever wants to be expressed on the page.

4. **Reflect.** Pause, ask a question that helps you inquire, and then write some more.
5. **Affirm.** Bring closure to your journaling time by giving thanks for your time to write and reflect.

May reflective journaling support you to live well and live inspired from within.

About the Author

Lynda Monk, MSW, RSW, CPCC, is the Director of the International Association for Journal Writing (IAJW.org). She is the co-editor of *Transformational Journaling for Coaches, Therapists, and Clients: A Complete Guide to the Benefits of Personal Writing* (2021). She is co-author of *Writing Alone Together: Journalling in a Circle of Women for Creativity, Compassion and Connection* (2014). She is the author of an ebook, *Life Source Writing: A Reflective Journaling Practice for Self-Discovery, Self-Care, Wellness and Creativity* (2009). She regularly speaks and teaches about the healing and transformational power of writing.

CHAPTER 6

The Creative Journal

By Lucia Capacchione

"Be patient board all that is unsolved in your heart and try to love the questions themselves like locked rooms and like books that are written in a very foreign tongue.... Live the questions now. Perhaps you will then gradually, without noticing it, live along some distant day into the answer."

—Rainer Maria Rilke

In 1973, after several years of crisis, I came down with a mysterious illness that doctors could not diagnose. I was getting sicker by the day. The doctor's hit-and-miss medication approach led to a long list of side effects. Bed-bound in a pre-internet era, with no TV in my room, I read many books to keep boredom at bay, including Anaïs Nin's *Diary*. It was a stressful time of endless days and sleepless nights, full of changing symptoms, extreme fatigue, anxiety, and uncertainty.

As a professional artist, my go-to was my sketchbook, where I combined inspirational quotes from famous people with my own images. This was always a place of creative exploration and expression. As I was journaling in my sickbed, I began to write out my own words. Feelings, observations, reflections, and dreams spontaneously poured out onto the page. This was not my normal use of my sketchpads; it just happened. Soon drawings to illustrate the words flowed out. The images looked strange and unfamiliar. They were unlike anything I had ever created as an artist and were not "art." They made no sense to me and were reminiscent of artwork by the mentally ill I'd seen on an art department field trip in college. I thought I was losing my mind.

I kept journaling because there was nothing else to do. I realized that every time I did it, I felt a little better. One of my friends pointed out to me that my style of journaling was like art therapy. Another friend recommended her therapist, Ms. Bond Wright, a highly creative practitioner of body-mind healing, Gestalt therapy, and transactional analysis. When I felt strong enough, I pursued therapy with her, which led to my next big breakthrough. Ms. Wright had me print with a big kindergarten crayon on large newsprint pads using my nondominant hand (the one I do not normally write with). The goal was to experience the inner child state directly through printing with the unschooled hand. It was slow and awkward, and I felt like a four-year-old. It was magic! This process freed up my feelings, energy, creativity, and inner wisdom in a way I'd never experienced.

One day while journaling at home, my left hand inadvertently grabbed the pen and quickly drew a stick figure of a little girl. The drawing looked like it had been created by a four-year-old. Then the little girl in the drawing spoke. She printed out her feelings in bold block letters. What followed was a powerfully written dialogue between both hands. The voice of my assertive inner child flowed through my nondominant hand. In contrast, my dominant hand spoke for my negative inner critic, who immediately put the child down.

A confrontation ensued: the critic lost to the inner child. This was followed by a paragraph of introspective writing, done with my dominant hand, containing deep insight into the *meaning* of my illness. It was a rebirth. More importantly, I realized I had just discovered the cause (self-judgment) and the cure (creative inner child) for creative blocks. I had let my rational, linear left brain *know* what my emotional and creative right brain was *feeling*. Within six months of starting to journal, I had my health back. My exploration continued with two-handed drawing, in which I scribbled with both hands at the same time. This was always relaxing and brought about a sense of calm and well-being.

When I shared some of my journal pages with a friend, she said, "Lucia, you've been doing art therapy in your journal. Have you thought of becoming an art therapist?"

I said, "You mean basket weaving in mental hospitals? That's not for me!"

Then she explained what art therapy was: psychotherapy in which the unconscious is accessed through spontaneous art and discussed with a therapist.

I said, "Yes, that's exactly what I'm doing. Except for the talking to the therapist part. I'm *writing* the words down in my journal."

After recovering from my illness, I entered a master's degree program, joined the American Art Therapy Association, and became a registered art therapist.

In my private practice, which opened in 1976, I developed my Inner Child Reparenting Method. I also taught a class called "The Creative Journal" in local colleges and YWCA. In these classes I shared prompts based on my journal processes. Soon students began healing chronic or serious illnesses and uncovering deep wells of hidden talent in art and writing. When they clamored for a book of journal prompts, my career as an author was born. Illustrated by my students and clients, *The Creative Journal: The Art of Finding Yourself* was published in 1979.

I conducted evidence-based research on The Creative Journal in the classroom in public elementary schools in California (Garvey Schools, 1981–82) and Texas (Edinburg Schools, 2014). The method proved to strengthen academic skills, reduce behavioral problems, enhance social-emotional learning, and relieve symptoms of test anxiety. Based on this research, I authored a series of *Creative Journal* guides for children, teens, and parents. In 1997, I co-founded an international educational program for professionals with Dr. Marsha Nelson. Creative Journal Expressive Arts (CJEA) certification training prepares educators, therapists, and mental and health care professionals to teach, counsel, and coach using my methods.

Twenty-two books have followed, including *The Power of Your Other Hand* and *Recovery of Your Inner Child*, which are used by many professionals working with clients. The Creative Journal Method has been implemented in large school systems (pre-kindergarten to twelfth grade), universities, hospitals, Veterans Administration programs, prisons, and more. My Visioning® life coaching method integrates collage vision boards with journal processes. My Body-Mind Healing-Arts Method, integrating journaling and all the arts, has been used in support groups for healing trauma, addictions, cancer, and other life-threatening or chronic illnesses.

Let me tell you a little about Creative Journal Expressive Arts principles and practices. CJEA is a method with simple tools that help with healing, creativity, and life Visioning®. If you can hold a crayon, you can do this work. It's appropriate for all ages, from toddlers to seniors, and for all populations, regardless of your zip code or community. There are professionally certified CJEA practitioners worldwide applying these methods in a variety of cultures and settings.

CJEA methods are used internationally in mental health care, addiction treatment, body-mind healing, education, life and career coaching, creativity, spiritual guidance, education, and more. CJEA Methods use a drugless prescriptive approach, guiding individuals with prompts tailored to their needs. Here are a few headlines:

Privacy and Confidentiality

The Creative Journal Method puts honesty and freedom of expression first. For this reason, journals need to be private and kept in a safe place, free from judgment and criticism by others.

Sharing

Selective sharing can be done, but only with people who are emotionally safe (accepting and nonjudgmental), such as a therapist, spiritual counselor, or loved one.

Frequency

One doesn't have to make entries every day; however, a regular practice yields greater benefits.

Time for Journaling

To develop a regular journaling practice, it is best to make time and space each day or week. Giving yourself the gift of privacy and quiet time for self-reflection, inner exploration, and creative expression is one of the most important benefits of journaling.

Date the First Page

Date the first page of each journal entry so that you can track your inner journey.

Journal Review

Revisiting your journals can reveal patterns and trends in one's life. A journal review can unearth early warning signs and encourage us to act. Looking back at where you have been can reveal the progress you've made.

Supplies

- Unlined blank book (preferably 8.5 x 11 in) or unlined bond paper in a three-hole punched binder
- Thin tipped colored pens, wide markers, crayons (twelve colors or more of each)
- Collage materials (optional): magazines, personal photos/snapshots, colored paper, scissors, glue, or glue sticks

Try This

Some Basic Journal Prompts

- **Feelings.** How do you feel right now? Draw your feelings out with your nondominant hand. Scribbles, abstract shapes, symbols, and images are all fine.
- **Talking Pictures.** If it could talk, what would your drawing say? Write with your nondominant hand. Each element or color may have its own message.
- **Current Challenge.** With your nondominant hand, draw a current challenge in your life. It can be a doodle, abstract shape, or recognizable image.
- **Dialogue with the Drawing** of the current challenge. The dominant hand writes the questions (your voice), the nondominant hand answers (speaking for the picture). Questions: *Who or what are you? How do you feel? Why do you feel that way? What do you need from me? (Optional) What are you here to teach me?*
- **Creative Block Buster.** With your dominant hand, write out what your inner critic says to you. Use the second person only. Example: *You're no author. You can't write. Look at this stuff you've written. It's a mess ... You're wasting your time. No publisher is ever going to publish this.*

- **Sassing Back.** Using your nondominant hand, let your assertive, creative child sass back. *I'm going to do it anyway in spite of you ... You're the one who is wasting your time. Get lost, will you?* (This dialogue from my journal broke me through a paralyzing creative block while working on my first book, *The Creative Journal.*)

I hope you'll enjoy this method and find it useful!

About the Author

Lucia Capacchione, PhD, A.T.R., R.E.A.T., is an art therapist and bestselling author of twenty-three books, including *The Creative Journal, The Power of Your Other Hand*, and *Recovery of Your Inner Child.* She was an early pioneer in journal therapy, inner child work, and expressive arts therapy in the 1970s. She has originated unique approaches to well-being and creativity. Her Creative Journal Expressive Arts (CJEA) method is used internationally in mental health care, addiction treatment, body-mind healing, education, life and career coaching, creativity, spiritual guidance, education, and more. She is the director of the CJEA professional certification training program for counselors, teachers, and coaches. She lives in Cambria, California.

CHAPTER 7

The Storytelling Journal

By Judy Reeves

"The universe is made of stories, not of atoms."

—Muriel Rukeyser

Humans have been telling stories since language was invented. Stories are not only how we communicate and entertain, but stories are how we learn. Lisa Cron, in *Wired for Story*, writes, "Story, as it turns out, was crucial to our evolution—more so than opposable thumbs. Opposable thumbs let us hang on; story told us what to hang onto." Our brains are hardwired to respond to story, and so it is no wonder there is the possibility of story in everything we write, from our grocery lists and to-do lists to our letters and social media posts, and for those of us who are journal-keepers, in our journals.

Our stories connect us as human beings and connect us to ourselves. They are the most fundamental way we organize and store information; they are how we make sense of the events of the world.

Scott Russell Sanders calls stories "the most human art" and gives us ten reasons we'll always need a good story. From creating community and engendering compassion, stories show us the consequences of our actions and educate our desires. Stories help us dwell in place and time; they help us deal with suffering, loss, and death; they teach us how to be human. Sanders writes, "Stories give us hope of finding meaning within the great mystery."

We are natural storytellers; we simply can't help ourselves. Meet a friend in the produce section of the grocery store, and we say, "Guess what happened!" Our eight-year-old comes home from school and we ask, "How was school today?" Begin any sentence with "I remember..." and you'll proceed from memory into story.

"We tell stories every day—mostly to ourselves," wrote film director Mark Travis. "We tell ourselves stories to make a point, to imagine a possible future, to remind ourselves, to reprimand ourselves, to comfort ourselves."

I've just opened an ancient journal of mine to August 20, 1990. The first line reads, *A compartment to myself; how lovely.* Many other entries, too many to name, begin with the weather. But how we perceive the weather can be a story in itself:

> *The sun is shining today and ...*
> *I wish the rain would stop...*
> *What a storm!*

We continue from there. This is the weather, and this is how it affected me, and that becomes a story. We record in our journals what matters to us, what we notice, what we care about, what we worry about, what we're attempting to understand about ourselves and others. When we try to make sense of our lives, we naturally shape our thoughts and ideas into narrative, which is to say, into story.

Now, before you read any further, open your journal and see where you've told yourself a story or the beginning of one. It may not look like what you might consider a "story," no "once-upon-a-time" opening, no classic first line, no "Call me Ishmael," or "It was the best of times; it was the worst of times." But wherever you begin, as you write, you have begun a story.

Another entry from my journal, this one the most recent:

Sunday, March 7.

Sometimes you just want to sit with coffee and look out the window.

When we consider the journal as storyteller, we can view it from two perspectives:

1. **Journal as listener.** This is where we tell our stories, record them, and write what's on our minds, whether a major life event or an observation that the sun is shining. When we write, our words may help us understand something about ourselves, the effects of an experience, or the meaning of an interaction or a dream. These are the stories that connect us to ourselves.

2. **Journal as storyteller.** Within these pages reside the source for stories we may want to extract, rewrite, and enlarge into a personal narrative essay or scene or fragment of a memoir or to use as the seed from which to grow a fictional story or novel. These are the stories that can connect us with others.

Journals I kept thirty years ago, throughout a seven-month solo trip across Europe and to India, were invaluable as I wrote a memoir of that time. I selected bits and pieces recorded in the journals and reshaped them, uncovering, recovering, and discovering the true story of the journey and how it affected the person I am today. In the translation, I rewrote the story in a public voice versus the private voice I used in my journal. I didn't include the day-in and day-out mundane notes that my journals sometimes contained. Neither did I use the pages and pages of internal examination and rumination, though these revealed my emotions, which shaped the re-visioning. I did use dates and facts and descriptions of people, places, and things. Sometimes I copied word for word, but not often. Simply put, the story could not have been told as thoroughly, with as many specific details, nor as deeply honest, without the material from the journals.

As an example of how a journal entry can be the source for a fictional story, I came across this single line in one of my old journals:

Ted sent an email today that said, "Let's take a couple hundred and head out, see how far we get."

Using that line as a starting point led to a fun and playful story that had nothing to do with the "real" Ted, which was an entirely different story.

Rereading old journals from the perspective of storyteller in search of material can be a sentimental journey down memory lane, the patient dig of an archeologist in a historical site, or a canoe ride along the river of life with all its curves and bends, its rapids and calm, its depths and shallows. If you choose to take the journey, a few suggestions to consider in rereading:

- Decide if you want to focus on a particular time—months, years, decades. You can read chronologically to determine the progression of story over time or dip in at random for surprises.

- Set aside time when you can be uninterrupted for a few hours or longer. Consider a day or weekend or even longer "retreat," where you can focus on reading, reviewing, making notes. I have a ritual of spending New Year's Eve rereading my journals of that year.

- Create a note-taking or marking system to help organize the material. I use different colored sticky notes to identify various categories—blue for possible narrative essays, yellow for memories that might be part of a memoir, pink for potential fiction, green for recurring themes (which, in their repetition, may inspire a deeper dive into a particular story). I also use highlighters to mark sections within the journals themselves. I always have a notebook nearby to write notes on which I may want to follow up—reconnecting with someone, finally reading a book I made mention of, remembering a quote or play or movie.

Try This

Going forward, as you continue your journaling practice, some suggestions that may enrich your journal's storytelling voice:

- **Write specific details:** The names of people, places, and things. Write the kind of bird that sings outside your window at the Airbnb you've taken on your vacation. Note the place you had lunch with your old friend and what you ate. What's the book you're reading now, the song playing in your head?

- **Use concrete descriptions:** Write bungalow or Craftsman or Spanish style, rather than just "house." Say chocolate raspberry mousse instead of merely "dessert." A willow, not just a tree; red geraniums rather than flowers (and give the red its name, too).

- **Do a sensory inventory:** Write what you see, hear, taste, smell, touch. Include light, air, atmosphere, and mood. Color them and shape them with lively detail.

- **Capture dialogue:** Who said what to whom. Note: eavesdropping is allowed, even encouraged.

- **Describe others:** Tall? How tall? In comparison to what? Eyes? What color? What does it remind you of? Here's a line from Margaret Atwood's novel, *The Edible Woman*. "She wore her usual Betty Grable hairdo and open-toed pumps, and her shoulders had an aura of shoulder pads even in a sleeveless dress."

- **Use concrete words rather than abstract ones:** I read once that "it's harder to write about God than to write about God's hat." Writing our emotions takes us into murky territory. How do you describe love? What can you say about anger? What are the words for sorrow? This is where the common advice, "show, don't tell," comes in and where, as writers—in journals and otherwise—we must slow down and go inside the experience. Writing a small scene, describing what you might see in a snapshot of the event, or, as Anne Lamott suggests in her book *Bird by Bird*, write what you can see inside a one-inch picture frame. Showing the tender hand of a grandfather on the shoulder of his small grandson who is smiling up at him illustrates "love" in a way that brings the emotion of the word alive. As writers and storytellers, this is what we aim for.

- **Each day or each journal writing session, write one moment that mattered:** One surprise or astonishment or joy, large or small; one troubling thought or worry or concern for yourself or others or the world; one thing you know for sure which may or may not be true the next day; or one "I remember..." memory.

Journaling allows us to go deeper into story, especially if we slow down and take care to use the language of storytelling. Writing these stories, piecing them together, we come to better understand ourselves and make meaning of our lives, and who knows what stories our journals might tell others and thereby connect in a most human way.

About the Author

Judy Reeves is a writer, teacher, and daily journaler who has published four books on the craft of writing, including the award-winning, *A Writer's Book of Days*, and the critically acclaimed *Wild Women, Wild Voices*. Find her at judyreeveswriter.com.

CHAPTER 8

The Healing Journal

By Jacob Nordby

"Applying creativity to healing changed everything.
I believe that creativity in motion heals everything."

—SARK

The warehouse was dim and silent. I was all alone there—alone with my crazy, anxious thoughts and feelings. Thirty-five years old and suddenly upended by life. Just over a year before, I had been the CEO of my own company, respected by many as an upwardly mobile entrepreneur, and now I was laboring in a patchwork of part-time jobs just to keep food on our plates. What transpired to destroy the pretty picture is a story familiar to many who lived through the global financial disaster of 2008.

The thing is, this was happening to me. I was afraid, confused, and desperate about providing for my children; it was a personal crisis I was having at the moment. And I sensed that something much deeper was presenting itself then, too.

This looming wave of feelings was something I had been swimming hard to stay ahead of all my life. It was larger and older and more all-encompassing than a career crisis, than financial problems. I had handled those sorts of things before. What was this?

At the time, I didn't have the tools or skills to engage with the question. All I knew was that I was scared and in pain—I needed relief.

I looked at the copy of *The Artist's Way* lying nearby. A gift from my father, I hadn't paid it much attention until then. But some inner tug was responsible for making me grab it on my way out the door to work that morning. I opened it and began to read. Julia Cameron's words became a toe, nudging the door of my heart open a little, letting in a small amount of light. She seemed to know what it was like to start from a place of feeling lost, so I was willing to follow her instructions for a while. It couldn't hurt, could it?

> The bedrock tool of a creative recovery is a daily practice called Morning Pages... Morning Pages are three pages of longhand, stream of consciousness writing, done first thing in the morning.

I didn't know about a creative recovery, but any kind of recovery sounded wonderful.

So, I began.

Following those instructions to the letter at first, I wrote. And wrote. And wrote.

A kind of inquiry-dialogue developed in my notebook, pen moving faster and faster as the dam broke, and feelings I had suppressed for a lifetime poured onto the paper. Tears often fell on the page, blurring the ink as I wrote right through the spreading drops. It didn't matter. Something good was happening. In this space, I was safe to express everything, safe to say it exactly as I felt it, often using terrible grammar, profanity, and breaking every one of my perfectionistic rules.

And it was safe to be honest about the things I always hid from other people: anger at my previous business partners, sadness about surprising old memories that surfaced from childhood, fury about early abuse and neglect, self-reproach for the weakness and stupidity that seemed to be responsible for my plight...nothing was off-limits. I could ask any question, say any impolite, blasphemous thing, express all the unworthy feelings. In this space, everything was permitted—invited, even. And the liberation of it all was that nothing that happened there was wrong or shameful. The ticking bomb could go off and destroy nothing. What a relief!

I didn't know it at the time, but I was laying the foundation for healing and sanity much more solid and enduring than anything I had experienced in the outwardly respectable life I was previously living.

For more than a decade since then, Morning Pages have become my own pages. No longer strictly following Julia Cameron's instructions, I return to the journal repeatedly—morning, midnight, or afternoon—whenever I feel overwhelmed or anxious.

I'd like to invite you to try these simple writing practices that can help you hear the voice of your inner self again. When this happens, you will be astonished at times by what comes out. At other times, you are likely to laugh with some relief at seeing the stupid, cruel voices in your head spill out as ink on paper and realize that they are not your own—I know that I frequently do.

This begins the process of sorting and separating your true inner voice from the chatter of social conditioning and harmful beliefs. This practice also develops trust in who you are and confidence to navigate life according to what you desire.

As you experiment with the prompts, I encourage you to remind yourself of three things:

1. I am a writer. I can write to myself and express my feelings, needs, desires, and ideas clearly.

2. I'm writing this only for myself and to myself. It's not for anyone else to see, approve of, or criticize.

3. I don't need any validation from others in this space. I am learning to be my own best friend and ally.

Instructions

It's almost too simple. Your mind might do what mine often does—dismiss this as ineffective because it's not complicated. Can sitting down with nothing but a pen and a piece of paper for ten or twenty minutes every day and answering two or three basic questions do anything worthwhile?

While I can't answer that for you, *I'd like to invite you to try it.* Maybe you can tell your mind that this practice is supported by tons of research and many books by experts who know what they're talking about. My mind is a little bit snobby and gets a lot of comfort from things like that.

Try This

How to Begin

1. Get a notepad and pen.
2. Set aside ten minutes in a quiet place (if you feel like writing longer, please do—but ten minutes is a great way to start).
3. Write the answers to three questions.

Question One: "What Am I Feeling Right Now?"

Let yourself describe *any* feelings you have, including frustration with the process of writing anything down. This is where you get to be terribly honest. Don't try to be lofty, profound, wise, or kind. Let anything come out that wants to come out. If you feel bored, anxious, tired, afraid, curious, happy, sad… say so. Ask yourself why and let the answers come out on the page.

I encourage you to include physical sensations you're having—describe any discomforts or pain, talk about the small things in your immediate environment that feel good. For example, "I feel my butt nestled solidly in the chair here at Neckar Coffee Shop. My head aches a little because I stayed up too late last night, but the steam from my coffee is a promise that something hot and good will help."

Most of us are so disconnected from our physical selves that writing a few lines about what's happening around us can help create a more grounded sense.

Remember, nothing is too small or silly to write about. The only thing that matters is being honest with yourself.

Maybe you're wrestling with a tough relationship issue—a hurting friendship or romantic partnership, something with a parent or sibling, a worry about one of your children, or something interpersonal at work. Talk about it. Especially describe how you *feel* about it.

Question Two: "What Do I Need Right Now?"

Much like the first question, the only thing that matters now is that you let yourself tell the truth. Many of us are not in the habit of saying (or even knowing) our needs. This often started in early childhood, when a parent or caregiver (probably unintentionally) communicated to our young psyches that our needs were unimportant or even wrong. This tells a developing mind that having needs isn't safe, and it can take some time and dedicated effort to dismantle the old beliefs.

Begin to answer the question, "What do I need right now?" Start small and be honest. It might be something as simple as, "I need to pee." I suggest that you jump up and do that first before anything else happens. The practice of paying attention to your needs, acknowledging them, and meeting them as quickly as possible, is surprisingly therapeutic. It is an important part of the process of healing the connection to your inner creative self.

Questions One and Two are meant to get you going, and it doesn't matter where you start. Psychologically speaking, all roads can lead you home to yourself. Expressing the smallest, most shallow-seeming anxiety or desire can be a thread you pull that unravels a knotty issue in your life.

Question Three: "What Would I Love?"

This is a magical question in that it has the power to shift you into a state of possibility and imagination. I use it often in my personal practice and ask it at some point in nearly every personal guidance session with my clients.

I encourage you to pick one of the challenge items from Questions One or Two and ask this question. Write the answers without judgment or skepticism. If your mind is like mine, it might say something like,

"Well, *of course*, you'd love to give yourself a break and take a vacation to somewhere warm, but how's that going to happen when your kids need rides to college and you have metric tons of work to do? *Get real*."

The point of this question is to simply allow yourself to state what you would love in any given situation.

As you write the words, "I would love," and follow with a statement of an outcome or feeling you desire, you positively activate your imagination.

Question Three is an invitation to let yourself retrain your imagination so that your powerful subconscious mind can begin to turn your choices, behavior, and focus *toward* what you would love.

You can ask Question Three differently, too: "How would I love to feel?" This is often helpful when you're in a whirlwind of confusion, anxiety, or insecurity. "How would I love to feel?" Maybe the answer is, "I would love to feel calm and centered right now." You can follow up with, "How would that feel in my body?" This can lead to taking small actions such as breathing deeply, stretching, and reminding yourself of the truth: "I am safe. I am lovable. I am resourceful." I have often found that this one question can move me into a different state and help me see the next step forward rather than remain frozen in anxiety or confusion.

As I've refined this practice over the years, it has become a daily part of my life. I've shared it with thousands of people and asked mental health professionals for their input, too. Therapists tell me that they're using it with their clients as it makes the process of getting started with a journal so simple, and it complements other healing modalities or approaches.

Whether you use the process I've shared here or simply open your notebook and write whatever is top of mind for you, I know that something powerful happens.

I promise you that if you use this simple pattern of questions, you will discover that you have developed a new relationship. You will heal and strengthen your connection to your inner creative self. As this happens, you will notice that your daily session isn't a chore; it's a conversation with a best friend: you.

This best friend never gets tired of listening to you, no matter how often you repeat the same things day after day. This friend is wise and kind. Your inner creative self longs to become your ally in healing and creating a life that you love.

About the Author

Jacob Nordby is a writer living in Boise, Idaho. You might find him on a trail in the nearby foothills or writing away in the quietest corner of a coffee shop downtown. He is the author of several books, including his latest release, *The Creative Cure: How Finding and Freeing Your Inner Artist Can Heal Your Life.*

Learn more about his books, speaking, online courses, and creative guidance sessions by visiting www.jacobnordby.com

CHAPTER 9

The Legacy Journal

By Merle R. Saferstein

"The wisdom that comes with living is a gift to share."

—Merle R. Saferstein

Unlike journaling we do for ourselves, legacy journaling is written for the benefit of others. A legacy journal can be a record of one's spiritual values, life lessons, messages from the heart, reflections, and more. Legacy journaling provides the beneficiary with insight into someone else's thoughts and feelings. It serves as a first-person account of one's journey and contains a peek into one's soul and life. A journal we write for ourselves might eventually morph into a legacy journal.

The idea to create a legacy journal first came to me about twenty years ago, when I began to rethink what to do with my collection of then 350 journals. Before that, I was convinced I would leave these volumes to my children. However, as time passed, it became clear to me that I was writing for myself. In every volume, there was something I would never want anyone in my life to see. That's when I knew it would be a mistake to leave my journals to my children as it could have possible negative consequences that I would never intend.

Yet, I wanted to leave a written legacy for my loved ones and future generations. With that in mind, I undertook a project of great magnitude—

understanding that by doing this, I would be sharing the essence of who I am and my life's journey.

Imagine my collection of journals as a tapestry. Initially, I identified approximately seventy topics, which encompass the individual threads of my life. I have untangled them, so each subject is as a single strand apart from the rest. To look at marriage or parenting or any of the other subjects by themselves, without anything else encumbering them, gives me a microscopic, uninterrupted view of each of these threads and aspects of my life.

The process of my legacy writing involved reading each journal carefully and deciding which excerpts I wanted to share. I marked them with sticky notes. Once I completed an entire volume, I entered those selected excerpts into the computer according to the individual topics.

July 1, 2002

As I work, I am being careful not to include anything that would be hurtful to someone else. I'm sure there will be instances when it is key to the situation to mention a person or when leaving someone out would be inauthentic, but my intentions will be honorable. In some cases, if what I'm writing about is sensitive, I might substitute a pronoun or make up a name to protect the individual. In reality, it doesn't matter who the people are. What is important is what happened, the meaning it holds for me and what is to be learned.

July 22, 2002

My life comes back to me in vivid detail and in living color as I read what I wrote years before—moments that I had long ago tucked away. Re-examining my life from this perspective gives me a chance to look at things differently and see how I lived, what I thought and how I felt. It also helps me to see how I have grown, what I've learned and what has stayed the same. And above all else, it provides me with information that I can pass along to others.

July 9, 2005

Last night, I dreamed I was at the ocean. There was an amazing influx of shells, coral and sponges lining the shore. It was one of those magnificent days when abundant treasures were at my feet. I woke up thinking that this dream was about my journals and how all my pearls of wisdom are waiting to be discovered.

November 5, 2010

I have reconsidered and am now clear that I want a wider audience than just my children. Also, I'm looking at what the final product might be when I finish working on my legacy journaling project. I'm asking myself these questions to help me figure it out. What do I specifically want to share with just my children? What do I want to leave for my grandchildren as well as for my family and friends? Will it be the same as what I'd consider sharing with a broader audience? Should I just create one document for everyone?

December 24, 2010

The more progress I make, the more I realize the value in what I am doing and know that I will be leaving a rich legacy in some way. I also have become aware of how, while this is for the future generations in my life, what I am experiencing is first and foremost for me. When I initially began, I hadn't thought about the impact this would have on me as I walked back in my life. In some ways, it's a life review.

Having completed the initial process of selecting the excerpts from my journals, I am now whittling down each topic. Some have as many as 100–250 pages, and my goal is to reduce those to approximately thirty pages each. When I complete this phase, I will then put them together into a collection of three books. I plan to dedicate them to my children and grandchildren and publish them for a wider audience.

Living and Leaving Your Legacy®

Three years ago, during a *Living and Leaving Your Legacy*°class I was teaching at a cancer center, I met and became friends with a forty-year-old woman who had metastatic breast cancer. I encouraged her to journal and to make a legacy video for her three-year-old daughter. My friend fought hard to be cured so she could live to raise her child. Unfortunately, she died in September 2020.

Three weeks before her passing and while she was in hospice, her brother called me. She wanted him to ask if I would be willing to read her journals and choose those passages that I felt would be important for her daughter to have someday.

It was a stunning request that I readily agreed to do. Luckily, I had the opportunity to write to my friend while she was still alive. I let her know I was honored to do this and would choose excerpts I felt could be shared while carefully respecting her privacy.

Above all else, I was overwhelmed that she was entrusting me with her personal and precious journals. She would be gone, and I would be left with her most intimate, authentic thoughts and truths. I understood this to be a sacred responsibility. When I agreed, I knew it would not be emotionally easy to embark on creating her legacy journal but also thought it would be tremendously meaningful. More than anything, I wanted to make sure that her daughter would eventually receive as much as possible of her mother from these journals.

What I realized as I made my way through her journals is that it's one thing to read my own, but it's a completely different experience to read someone else's journals—especially since she wrote them, never intending for anyone else to ever read them.

There were ten journals in all. Some were notebooks, two were calendar journals, and the rest she had purchased or given to her as gifts. In one of them, she kept track of her medical issues, doctor's appointments, and medications. In some, she wrote notes from the various classes she was taking. She had specifically written one of the calendar journals for her daughter, and that one, of course, will be saved for her in its entirety.

This profound experience gave me a window into my friend's heart and soul. I understood that I would be preserving her legacy, which to me is the ultimate in legacy journaling. It also allowed me to reflect on what matters most and pass along those life lessons, messages, values, and events for her daughter to cherish.

Try This

Legacy Journaling Tips

It's important to identify your intended audience for your legacy journal first. Deciding this will help you choose what is relevant to include.

Identify the themes you want to share. Then take excerpts/passages based on those themes as you read through your journals.

Edit and synthesize the text. Keep on refining until you have the product you want to pass on to your intended recipients.

Remember to keep in mind, when it comes to the creative process, there's no one "right way" to approach legacy journaling.

Different Forms of Legacy Journaling

Journal entries might be used with the following legacy projects and can be considered different forms of legacy journaling.

- **Legacy love letters:** Commemorate special occasions such as graduations, birthdays, weddings, religious rites of passage, and other special days with a legacy love letter. Share important sentiments, memories, wishes, stories, and values memorably and lovingly. By doing so, you honor the individual.
- **Ethical wills:** An ethical will, which links people to their future generations, is a spiritual document—the essence of one's life lessons, values and beliefs, hopes and dreams. It addresses people's universal needs to be remembered, know that they matter, and pass

along messages for future generations. The ethical will, which is to be read as a hopeful, positive piece, is intended to be written for future generations to learn from and cherish.

- **Journals:** Write a journal specifically for someone. For example, one might begin a journal when a grandchild is born and continue writing in it throughout their life.
- **Memoirs and autobiographies:** Writing about one's life as a memoir or an autobiography is a way to share our personal story.

Above all else, a legacy journal in any form is a gift to the person who writes it and a gift to those fortunate enough to receive it.

About the Author

Merle R. Saferstein is an author, legacy educator, and former director of educational outreach at a Holocaust center. She lectures and teaches legacy to audiences locally, nationally, and internationally. Merle trains hospice staff and volunteers to help patients leave their legacies and works with patients at the end of their lives doing sacred legacy work. She is an IAJW council member, facilitates journaling circles, and has taught journaling to bereaved children, adults, students, and teachers. Merle can be reached at MerleRSaferstein.com or merles1212@gmail.com.

CHAPTER 10

The Elemental Journal

By Midori Evans

"Everything was simple, physical, painful, exalting.
The world consisted of the four elements—
land and water, firepower and distancing air."

—Susan Sontag

Earth. Air. Fire. Water.

The very nature of our world, the four elements structure both our physical world and serve as a framework for our experiences. To explore them deeply creates a tether; our bodies are created of these elements, as is the world we inhabit. We can dive into the stories of our lives through an elemental framework.

On the winter solstice in 2020, Saturn and Jupiter seemed to come together in the sky in the "Great Conjunction." Students of astrology will tell you that the Great Conjunction marked a shift into a new era focused on increased innovation, mobility, and change. Absent an astrological interpretation, the events of 2020 brought upheaval on a scale few of us have ever lived through. What do these shifts mean in our lives? How do we relate to these basic elements and what can we explore in our daily journaling that helps us connect to them in a meaningful way?

Whether you view the four elements through an astrological lens, the scientific lens of the four properties of matter, or a spiritual lens for use in medicine wheels and sacred ceremonies, Earth, Air, Fire, and Water weave together the essence of our lives. Various traditions link emotional experiences, personality characteristics, and life choices to them; by following this elemental journaling practice, you create your own links, paths, and healing journeys.

Earth

To be grounded. To feel one's feet on the earth. To know that the land supports, feeds, and sustains us. To write of the element of earth is to tap into the energy of our entire ecosystem. You can build a new lattice of connections with the earth as you write.

Picture solidity. Focus on the physical body. Think of the strength and flexibility of saplings, reeds, and seedlings that are shooting up straight into the sky as they grow, their roots anchored in the earth.

Picture abundance. The earth feeds us and serves as our home. We erect structures, dig down for planting, and relish the extraordinary beauty that emerges.

Picture density. Though the hot magma core of our earth is liquid, we experience the earth as solid, dense, and unshakeable.

- **Earth Journaling Prompt 1:** Imagine life as a creature that never lands. Are you a seed, blown by the wind for eternity? Are you a sky denizen, floating on clouds or carried by star trails? In your writing, explore what the loss of the supportive earth would be like.
- **Earth Journaling Prompt 2:** Go outside to a place where you can feel some dirt. Even a small patch will do, or if you have indoor house plants, you can work with that. Dig down into the dirt with your hands. Allow the soil to sit in your palm and let your fingers feel the sensation of being immersed in the dirt. Journal about your experience of connecting with the earth.

Air

When you hear "air," what is your first thought? Is it of sky, breath, clouds, or being? How do you experience this intangible, imperceptible element? Does air hold any movement? Does it soar?

To take a breath of air is to breathe life, inhale movement, experience in our cells the constant changing of who we are, our environment, life. To write of air is to explore the currents of a day, see how our emotions flow and move and shift in little bits of time. Have you ever woken in the morning and thought: *here is my breath*? Have you ever walked outside and thought: *here is the first breath of outside air entering my lungs*?

- **Air Journaling Prompt 1:** How do you interact with air as breath? Write of the transformative process that happens as you take air into your lungs.
- **Air Journaling Prompt 2:** Choose a windy day for this prompt. Go outside to a wide-open space like a park, a big city intersection, or a field. Bring your notebook. Stand in one place for ten minutes and watch how the wind affects the objects in your environment. What do you observe?

Fire

To be with fire is to be with warmth, passion, and destruction. This vital element carries within it a real hint of danger, for when out of control, fire wreaks havoc, sometimes in the blink of an eye. It also exudes the power of brilliance as it sparks and brightens. What other messages do you hear when you think about fire?

Begin by picturing the associations you have with the element of fire. Go back in time to when fire warmed early humans living as hunter-gatherers. Stretch to today, with news images of fires out of control in the West of the United States, Australia, and beyond. For centuries, humans have used fire to understand the role of a controlled burn or of some plants' need for fire to be able to seed.

Think of fire as seeding elemental pieces of your life. Write about this. In what parts of your life would fire allow you to lay down some old wood, kindle a seed hidden deep in a pinecone, and restart an elemental process for you?

- **Fire Journaling Prompt 1:** Light a candle in your house. Watch the flame carefully, from a distance. Choose elements of the fire to focus on. First, watch the colors. Do you see the yellows, the blues, the dark rich browns? Then, watch the shape of the fire as it moves. Describe what you see.

- **Fire Journaling Prompt 2:** Images of fire can be powerful. If you need to, do some grounding exercises before attempting the following writing prompt. Use your imagination to envision the destruction of a forest fire. Begin with the fire racing through a forest, illuminating and burning trees from within. Move from there to imagining the crackling and bursting open of seed pods. Extinguish the fire and write about the new seeds being welcomed into the burnt ground.

Water

The dynamism of water and its extraordinary states can be the filter for our writing process about water. Liquid: pools of water, drops from a kitchen faucet, small puddles left over after a rainstorm. Frozen: ice cubes in our freezer, slivers of ice at the beginnings of a cold day, ice pictures etched on our windows. Gaseous: steam moving as we boil water for coffee, fog creeping across a morning meadow, our breath on a cold day.

In its liquid form, water flows much like our daily lives. Imagine welcoming the movement of water into your writing practice, perceiving its shifts. Where is the water pooling today? Where is water crashing over a causeway, running rapids, or sitting still as a mountain pool in winter?

- **Water Journaling Prompt 1:** Write about the movement of water in as many situations as you can think of. Describe ripples in a pond, circles expanding outward from a dropped stone, waves in a bay, or crashing upon a rocky shore. Watch the action, notice the water, see, and write.
- **Water Journaling Prompt 2:** Imagine a body of water you know well. Describe the water when the weather is calm and tranquil, and then describe it when a storm hits. Where does the water go? How far does its boundary expand? Experience the water moving, transforming; capture this energy in your writing.

Try This

The richness of the four elements can feed your writing practice in diverse and exciting ways. Create your own elemental journal by designing a mix of exercises from the following four categories.

Natural World

A myriad of opportunities exists to explore each of the four elements in the natural world. Almost any experience in nature provides nurturing or challenging material for an elemental journal entry. The natural world awaits our attention! Choose one element to focus on and use your five senses to describe what you experience. Locate local water sources and find places where you can interact with air differently, like a wind tunnel in a city or a rooftop. If you are stuck for inspiration, try making word maps; for example, fire can lead to stars, leading to meteor showers, and more. Write freely about your experience of focusing on the element and your senses.

Your Elemental Experiences

The focus here lies in how you interact with the four elements. On a purely physical level, how do you take the element into your body? How does your body interact with the elements, both outside and within your living space? Take a moment to make a list of the four elements in your daily life. Some examples include fire: cooking; air: boiling water; earth and water: watering the plants. Then write of what you notice in your physical body. Does your body change? Does the element change? What do you learn as a human interacting with the foundational elements?

Reading and Literary Exercises

Authors and poets have extolled the beauty of the natural world from time immemorial. Find a poem, a literary passage, or a travelogue that speaks to you. Read carefully to see what language the writer uses to describe the elements. What resonates for you in the writing? Connect it to something you see in your environment and see what emerges in your journal entry.

Shifts in the External Elemental Experiences

Life is in constant flux, and the human experience captures the mystery of the unknown. The focus here lies in watching the elements as they change and shift. Sit and listen to the wind on a windy day from four different locations. Repeat this same sitting and listening on a rainy day. Watch a video of a fireworks display to observe the light shifts in the sky. Choose an outdoor spot and monitor changes you observe over time. How does the interplay of earth, air, fire (light), and water change subtly or dramatically?

About the Author

Midori Evans is the founder of Midori Creativity (Midori Creativity: Creativity Consulting), a creativity-coaching business that helps individuals and businesses connect to their best creative selves. A lifelong creative explorer, Midori loves to travel and is a gifted writer, photographer, musician, and educator. She draws on the inspiration of the natural world in her work as a creativity coach, writer, and landscape photographer. She founded Creativity Abloom, a series of conversations about creativity, and currently runs Artists Share! (Artists Share), a monthly artist critique group, and seasonal Artist's Way group classes (Artist's Way). Look for her creativity exercises in *The Creativity Workbook for Coaches and Creatives* edited by Eric Maisel (http://bit.ly/2myCCWx).

CHAPTER 11

The Digital Journal

By Hannah Braime

"Documenting little details of your everyday life becomes a celebration of who you are."

—Carolyn V. Hamilton, *Art Improv 101: How to Create a Personal Art Journal*

The explosion of digital tools and hardware, plus their integration into our lives, has changed the way we live and work. It's also revolutionized the way we can journal. In this chapter, I invite you into the world of digital journaling and explore some of the many things you can do with a computer, smartphone, or tablet to record your life, savor memories, support your mental health and feed your creativity.

I've been using digital journaling in one form or another for over ten years. A lot has changed in that time: gone are the days when my digital journal was a jumble of disorganized word processor files. Now, there are apps where I can store photos, create video montages of my kids' daily lives, write while I'm out walking or running errands, and record voice memos. Digital journaling isn't limited to just written or spoken words. There are now many tools—tablets, styluses, and apps—that support digital art journaling. The possibilities with digital journaling are already plentiful and continue to expand all the time. Later in this chapter, I will share some specific techniques and ideas you can use in your digital journal. First, I want to give you an overview of digital journaling and some advantages and considerations involved in using digital journaling tools.

What Is Digital Journaling?

Simply put, digital journaling is journaling that uses technology. This might be a computer, a smartphone, or a tablet. You might use specialized journaling apps or more general writing software. Your digital journal can include written entries, photos, voice recordings, or videos. As I mentioned above, it can also incorporate art journaling. Unlike keeping a regular journal, you might find that you use several different journaling tools. I use a dedicated journaling app with multiple written and photo journals. I also use another app to create video montages using one second of video from my day. In the past, I have also used yet another app (a PDF editor) to keep a digital bullet journal and a website that promotes a digital version of Julia Cameron's Morning Pages (a practice of stream-of-consciousness writing she describes in her book *The Artist's Way*).

My digital journaling practice began in earnest when I moved countries several years ago. Unable to take my journals with me and with nowhere to store them, I decided to digitize them to keep my old entries. The mind-numbing weeks of scanning each notebook page-by-page that followed strengthened my resolve to go fully digital! And, as I delved further into the weird and wonderful world of digital journaling, I discovered far more than practical benefits.

The Benefits of Digital Journaling

One of the major benefits of taking your journal digital is flexibility. As well as being able to include a multitude of different formats and mediums, you can also journal wherever you are and whenever you like. Waiting in line? The perfect opportunity to jot down a few ideas. Captured by a beautiful sight while out and about? Record a quick video. Struck by a brilliant idea while exercising? Leave your future self a breathless voice memo.

In addition, most journaling apps also sync between devices, meaning entries you make on your phone show up on your laptop and vice versa. Keeping all my notes, thoughts, and ideas together in one application is easier than having different ideas scattered through different journals. In my digital journal, I have different notebooks and tags that allow me to organize and group my entries, but they are all in one place and easily searchable. I have multiple journals, including a journal for personal entries, a reading journal, a crafting journal where I record notes and photos of finished crafting projects and more, all of which are available at the touch of a button.

This brings us to another advantage of digital journaling: backups. If you lose your physical journal, that's it. It's gone. Even if a kind stranger returns it, did they read it? Did someone else find it in the meantime? Journals are private spaces, and I always found it hard to move past the fact that if I were to lose my notebook, someone—or multiple people—might have access to my most private thoughts and feelings. Obviously, privacy is a consideration when choosing a digital journal too, and I cover this more below, but the ability to sync and backup my journals gives me peace of mind. If I lose my phone or computer, it's a costly mistake, but I know I will be able to access my journaling entries again.

I discovered an unexpected benefit of using a digital journal when I learned that keeping one makes it easy to track metadata. For example, with each entry in my digital journaling application, the app will also record the location I made it, the weather, and—if I connect it to other applications—additional information like what music I've been listening to that day. Over time, it's been lovely to look back at journal entries from years ago, especially ones I made in different countries, and see exactly where I was and the weather that day. Even these minor details evoke stronger memories of that time than I otherwise would have.

You can also use this kind of data tracking for Quantified Self—tracking aspects of our daily life through technology. Depending on the journaling application you're using, you can import data from step trackers and set up daily prompts to record your mood. This can give you useful information about your habits that can help you make data-based adjustments toward a healthier and happier lifestyle.

As well as the above, there are plenty more automations and integrations you can use with digital journaling programs. You can log your social media entries and record which TV programs you've watched automatically, all without needing to make an entry yourself. This kind of automation is for the more technically minded user (it's not something I have set up myself), but I share it here to give you an idea of further possibilities. A wonderful feature of keeping a digital journal is that the possibilities are almost endless; the more you use it, the more you will find different ways of using it. And, if you can imagine it, someone somewhere has probably made a shortcut for it!

Considerations for Digital Journaling

Of course, there are considerations that come with digital journaling too. With all this personal data involved, the number one concern that comes to mind for most people is privacy. This is justified; most of us (myself included) don't truly understand the workings of, or our vulnerabilities to, modern evils like data privacy violations, so how can we trust that our journaling entries will be safe?

When choosing my digital journal, I opted for software that includes end-to-end encryption. This means any data from my journal stored on the developer's servers is encrypted and it appears as scrambled code. No one can view it without a unique key, which only I have access to. The downside of this is that if I lose my personal key (a combination of numbers and letters, like a long password), I also lose access to my journals.

Another drawback of digital journaling is that it can feel less personal. Staring at a backlit screen, reading your words back in a default font rather than your own handwriting can create a disconnect for some people that is hard to overcome. This is why I am a big advocate of using other mediums like photos, videos, and digital art journaling too. These capture visceral memories and help replace that personal connection to my entries that might otherwise feel lost.

Mixing and Matching Paper and Digital

As I mentioned earlier in this chapter, I started my digital journaling while traveling. Nowadays, my life is much more static, so have I gone back to paper?

Yes, and no. I still value the many benefits digital journaling offers that pen and paper can't. I also missed writing by hand. Today, I use my paper journal as a bullet journal, mapping out goals, plans, to-do lists, and so on. My digital journal has become a space for long-form reflection and deeper processing. In short, my paper journal has become more about "doing," while my digital journal is more about "being."

If the last few years are any indication of what's coming, soon we will have even more ways to record the moments and information that are most meaningful to us, including possibilities we can't even imagine right now. As more technology becomes available to digital journalers, one thing is certain: this is just the beginning.

Try This

- **Set up multiple journals for different topics or themes.** Options you might consider are a reading journal, a watching journal, or a journal for family members where you record specific memories and milestones related to them.
- **Try experimenting with different formats.** You can try photos, audio, video, and written entries.
- **Start a "three good things" journal.** At the end of each day, write three good things that happened that day. Reflect on this journal whenever you need a mood boost or a reminder of all the good things in life!

- **Try digital morning pages.** Using the app of your choice, write 750 words of stream-of-consciousness journaling.
- **Try automating the recording of certain information.** If your digital journaling app allows, try setting up an automated record of aspects like the day's weather and your location when you make the entry. As you look back on these entries, how does that additional information change your memory and experience of reflection?

About the Author

Hannah Braime is the author of several books about personal growth and creativity, including *The Year of You: 365 Journal Writing Prompts for Creative Self-Discovery*. She also shares psychology-based articles and resources on creating a meaningful life with greater courage, compassion, and authenticity at www.becomingwhoyouare.net.

CHAPTER 12

The Planning Journal

By Jennifer Britton

"Planning is bringing the future into the present
so that you can do something about it now."

—Alan Lakein

Planning journals provide an opportunity to pause, capture ideas, and track results. In today's digital space, planning journals provide a space to capture visual notes, synthesize, prioritize, and set direction. At the same time, disruption, change, and volatility require a different approach to planning. Let me explain.

Our world is shaped by what has been called the "attention economy," where we find ourselves constrained by a fixed amount of time and our limited attention span. Planning journals provide us with the opportunity to expand our thinking and increase our possibilities. Planning is an important process that allows us to pause, reflect, learn, and focus. Planning journals come in all shapes and sizes, from annual planners, to quarterly planners, to monthly planners, to weekly planners, to daily planners, and provide a visual window into our world at any given moment. They create a record of our lives and, whether used for business development or personal development, provide a centralized resource for tracking our progress.

Whether analog or digital, hard-copy or soft-copy, planning journals can be used to dream, set our direction, and prioritize our day. Planning journals provide the opportunity to see things "laid out" and visible, to prioritize what is most important to us and make strong decisions. Planning journals record events, helping us see what we've done, what we thought, who we met, and what we tried. Interesting patterns often appear when we take the time to reflect and review. This pause enables us to "look back in order to look ahead." Similarly, planning journals provide us with the opportunity to record our most important memories.

Plans are important for communication, productivity, and learning. Journals are important in helping us think through and explore ideas and issues that we may be facing. As a communication tool, planning journals help us distill ideas, synthesize concepts, and clarify our message. On a learning level, planning journals create a record and resource, which can capture achievements and identify learning. Ongoing learning is required for success in life and work and, with that in mind, reviewing our journals and our plans can help us unearth new layers of insights and possibilities.

In terms of getting things done, an old project management adage is, "Five minutes of planning can save up to one hour of unfocused effort." As it relates to projects, both career and personal, plans help us to:

- Set goals and objectives.
- Identify where we are and where we want to go.
- Consider what needs to get done.
- Identify risks and opportunities.
- Define the possible options we can take.
- Map out the journey from where you are to where you want to be.
- Stay on schedule and budget.
- Create a yardstick for measurement.
- Frame our success measures.
- Identify our learning.
- Distill lessons learned to be carried forward.
- Celebrate our successes.

Each of these can be a separate category of prompts in a planning journal. Each is a different pathway into the planning process. Within a planning journal are many different types of resources to support you, including:

- **Trackers.** Whether you want to track sales, steps, followers, or emails, trackers create a place to note metrics and actions taken. We don't always remember things as they happen, and trackers provide a valuable record to look back upon.
- **Content planners** help with planning and systematizing content creation. What would it be like to already have ideas for your content?
- **Weekly planners** help us focus on what's important each day.
- **Monthly planners** give us a snapshot of the month, while *quarterly planners* provide a wider view. What's important to note?
- **Annual planners** provide us with the "big picture" or 30,000-foot view. What are the big projects that you want to move forward?

Consider the level at which you want to plan. As Warren Wiersbe puts it, "You do not move ahead by constantly looking in a rearview mirror. The past is a rudder to guide you, not an anchor to drag you. We must learn from the past but not live in the past."

My Story

Influenced by thousands of hours of coaching individuals and business owners, in 2018, I embarked on creating and publishing two planning journals. The first, geared for professional coaches, is called *Coaching Business Builder* (CBB). It is a planner and workbook to support the planning, execution, and tracking around coaching business tasks and activities. In late 2018, in response to requests from my non-coach clients, I launched *PlanDoTrack* (PDT), a workbook planner for virtual and remote professionals. I often hear the following from people who use these planners:

- At the start: *"I have so much to do!"* Planners corral things and get them out of your head onto paper or the digital table. After: "Wow. That was so much easier to get things done."
- *"I don't know where to start!"* The daily practice of pausing to plan helps you prioritize, making the first steps clearer to see.
- *"I don't have time."* Many things don't take as much time when we can focus on them. The 21-for-21 Virtual Co-Working Sprints have shown how twenty-one minutes spent each day can quickly reduce the "running task list" when working in uninterrupted bursts.
- *"I don't know what I've done."* Weekly Reviews provide an opportunity to pause, take stock, learn, and adjust in thirty minutes or less.

Try This

Take your vision for this year (or the next three, five, or ten years) and chunk it down into more concrete steps. What's going to help you go from where you are to where you want to be?

Consider it in the *PlanDoTrack* buckets:

Plan

Create smaller milestones for your vision. Write out each one. What does that milestone look like? What is important to note around it? Note dates, resources, etc. Consider the level at which you want to plan. Your time window might be weekly, monthly, quarterly. What do you want to include sections around?

Do

Create a ritual. When do you want to do your planning regularly? Make it special. Do a weekly round-up of achievements and accomplishments. Write it down.

Track

What do you want to track? Identify the personal, entrepreneurial, or leadership elements you want to track, which might include:

- **Personal:** how much you walk, exercise, money you spend, etc.
- **Entrepreneurial:** sales made, clients served, new customers, website visits, etc.
- **Leadership:** one-to-ones held, time spent in meetings, results, key activities, etc.

What do you notice about the patterns?

A Few Tips

Schedule time for planning. Earmark time regularly for review and reflection. As PlanDoTrack asserts, "Daily Steps + Consistent Action = Momentum." It's the small steps that add up over time. Creating more strategic steps by focusing on what's important is valuable in an ever-changing environment. Write it down. Get your ideas, dreams, visions, and plans out of your head.

Consider the level at which it is useful to plan. Do you want to focus on content creation, tracking what you've done, or the weekly, monthly, quarterly, or annual view of your business?

Planning Journal Prompts

1. What areas could you benefit from doing more planning around?
2. Planning means to me...
3. My top three goals for this year are...
4. The one thing I want to make sure I accomplish this year is...
5. The Daily Steps I want to undertake toward my most important goal this year are...
6. I will track it by...

In closing, what regular practice of reflection, planning, action, and tracking will support you to do your best work, live your best life, or achieve your goals?

About the Author

Jennifer Britton is a long-time planning advocate. She's used journals throughout most of her life, from her years as a student, to working as a global leader with organizations including the United Nations. Her journals have provided an important record of her two decades as an entrepreneur and CEO. As a coach, Jennifer encourages her clients to use journals as a pause point. As a former project manager, she notes that journals are an important vehicle for productivity and results.

Jenn is the author of multiple business books, including *Effective Virtual Conversations*, and two planner workbooks, *Coaching Business Builder* and *PlanDoTrack*. Visit her online at www.PotentialsRealized.com or tune into her podcast, *The Remote Pathways*.

CHAPTER 13

The Altered Journal

By Chris Leischner

"Creativity defies precise definition."

—E. P. Torrance

I am a hit-and-miss kind of journaler. I can go for weeks not writing a thing, and then, in the middle of a walk or loading the washing machine, the urge hits me. I feel inspired, and I run to grab a scrap of anything to get the idea out before it disappears. I have often written on receipts or in book margins, on the back of envelopes, or even on my grocery list. Just getting it down helps me start a process of ruminating on my feelings or thoughts.

I had always thought that this meant I was not a journaling kind of gal. But I have come to understand that journaling is not prescriptive. I have no doubt that routine helps, but I do not do routine well, so I "catch is as catch can." I prefer to think of journaling as a process of coming to a place of awareness and exploration, letting your mind be curious, and going deep inside to find hidden spaces, whenever and wherever the ideas come to me. I have a bin full of bits and pieces that I am using to make up my major altered book journal, "The Book of My Life." This is a rather large undertaking when you have lived sixty-six years and have been keeping your scraps of paper for almost all those years.

The idea of altered book journals is a little backward, as most people find a lovely journal that speaks to their soul or sense of beauty. On the other hand, I collect these pieces of my narration and channel them into an already existing book, which I "alter" to fit the idea I have introduced in my scrap of thoughts. I take an old book and make it new again. This is not a new idea. Altered books have been around since the eleventh century when monks reused costly parchment by rubbing off ink or covering it over to reuse it again. This altered manuscript was known as a palimpsest and is the basis for altered book journals.

The book you choose to alter will become the container for your creativity. You can glue, cut, rip, punch, drill wire, stamp, fold, staple, embellish or paint your book. You take an existing hardcover book (these work best) and add and subtract groups of pages called *signatures*. Looking from the top of the spine, the book consists of several *signatures* bound together. When the book is opened in the middle of a signature, the binding threads can be seen. This is the type of book to use for your altered journal project. If you are a first-time "alterer," I suggest using a children's board book. The pages are already stiffened, and you do not have to remove any pages. Gently sand the pages to make them adhere better to acrylic paint, and you have a small journal for your first efforts.

Here are some tips. The paper should not be glossy. Choose a heavier, absorbent paper. First, open to the signature, with the thread showing, and take out the whole piece of paper. In standard books, these are approximately 8 x 11 inches in size when spread out and 4 x 5 when folded, depending, of course, on the size of the closed book. To create an anchor to insert a page, take a ruler and place it about ½-inch from the crease or middle of the signature and tear it off, leaving a piece to glue to without disturbing the signature. In general, paint first, glue next. I use a UHU glue stick, as it is acid-free and will stay glued for an exceptionally long time.

I leave the re-covering of the book for the end. You can also paint the cover if it is cloth. As you work, cover the entire two pages that are face-up as if they were one page. I use Gesso or heavier acrylics, but you can use crayons, felt pens, or watercolors. Remember to let them dry before gluing or writing on them. Now begin to build the page back again. You will need to put wax paper between the pages when you are working with a section. When you close it overnight, put some weight on the book to flatten it.

You can also embed your ephemera onto or into the page. Glue together pages with your ephemera piece in between. Cut or rip around the object to let it "break" through. Scrapbooking supplies have little glue dots you can use to affix the item to the page or cut into a group of pages to "embed" the object.

I use old gift wrap and ferry tickets to line the pages. Postcards make a great starting place for ideas, and dried flowers, when glued and covered with gel medium, remind you of the occasion when they were given or the feelings you had when they were received.

You can also stitch the pages together. Using a large darning needle and a blanket stitch, take four pages; fold the first two, top right corner to the signature's middle. You will see that when you stitch them together, you have a pocket for any number of things, pictures, cards as keepsakes, and ideas for writing.

I create around the words and form a context for the journal piece. It is a form of embodied creativity that goes beyond the written word to extend those feelings and thoughts into a piece of ephemera, recycled bits, loved art pieces, or just color, texture, and form. The choices are endless.

I found an old ledger from a Victoria loan company circa the 1930s. It was beautifully bound with leather corners and cloth covering. It has large, 11 x 14 pages covered with names and numbers of loan clients. I was saving it for something special when I read a book by Kate Morton called *The Clockmaker's Daughter*. Passages in this book spoke to me, releasing thoughts about my sense of place, time, and being. I began scribbling down thoughts and realized that this was the book that I would use for "The Book of My Life."

I gathered all the bits and pieces I had saved through the years, the entries in my notebooks, and the backs of scrap paper. I decided to organize them into nine chapters based on quotes from Kate's book. Into these nine chapters, I would fit my journal pieces. I called the chapters "What is Real to Me," "Belonging," "Place as Home," "Whose Truth is Real,"

"Permission," "Making a Difference," "Use Time Well," "What Speaks to Me," and "The Remainder." I chose nine chapters, as this is three threes or an infinity of infinity, a number that represents endlessness.

Each of these chapters is forwarded by a quote from the book and an attempt to put into context the entries that I have made. They are out of time, not following any linear order, but they connect who I am, or rather who I think myself to be. Though I have used art techniques and images throughout the altered book journal, the meat of this journal are my scraps of paper that contain my musings and memories. I do not copy them; I glue them in as-is.

There are many instructional books available on altered art and altered books. *Altered Art for the First Time* by Madeline Arendt is a good starting place and will give you lots of suggestions and tips for your journal. As you get more adventurous, you might want to try making your own books with the help of books like *Making Books and Journals: 20 Great Weekend Projects* by Constance E. Richards. Go to the Website of the International Society of Altered Book Artists (www.alteredbookartists. com). You will find how-to's, photos, and many suggestions for combining words and visuals into a journal experience that will stand the test of time.

Try This

An example of connecting written words, images, and the design for your page might be something like the following: *Journal about a turning point in your life.* Now focus on the words *turning.* What image comes to mind when you hear the word *turning*? I think of the hands of a clock turning around or a little girl turning circles until she is dizzy. What image can you find, create, or embed that captures the feeling of what you have written? Or take the word *point.* Does a picture of a hand pointing right at you come to mind, or does the sharp tip of a pencil circling round and round your words in and out back and forth make your point?

Do you have a symbol or sign that you put into every page that marks your words as yours, something besides your signature? I like to tuck a ladybug into my pages as it represents good luck and good fortune to me. It is a vibrant little creature that reminds me to smile and love my life.

Do you have a drawer full of cards from family and friends that you want to hold on to? Make yourself a card book but use each page to write about what the givers' thoughts and feelings mean to you.

You can create a poem or a visual piece by covering words with painters' tape and then using that color to cover the whole page. When the page has dried, you peel off the tape, and you have a new statement or poem or scattering of ideas.

Adding color, texture, and visuals can help you see things from a different perspective. Sometimes this helps us to step out of our comfort zone and use our creativity more.

Try a Round Robin for your altered book journal. Chose a theme and a book, then start with a page and your writing. Send the book from person to person so that each can be inspired and generate new ideas.

About the Author

Chris Leischner is a biophilic bibliophile. She began her love of paper, books, and words working in a printing company at the age of seventeen and has never stopped being entranced by the form and function of a book. She began altering books to avoid them getting thrown away and because her words needed a place to exist that reflected her love for saving the planet and reusing our resources. She has found that in altered book journaling, a place where words come home to comfortably sit in their own space of being. Repurposing old books into journals is her creative outlet for repurposing, reusing, and recycling old into usable again.

CHAPTER 14

The Becoming Unstuck Journal

By A M Carley

*"Being a writer means taking the leap
from listening to saying, 'listen to me.'"*

—Jhumpa Lahiri

After a lifetime of listening, do we now deserve to be listened to? Jhumpa Lahiri brilliantly invokes the bravery that every writer requires. From time to time, however, fear may attempt to silence us. The fear leads us to doubt our worthiness, and we can wind up feeling stuck and disconnected from our creative purpose. Journaling to the rescue! Over time, your journaling practice can help you maintain the connection to your sense of purpose that you need. It can also prevent creative stuckness from arising and reduce its impact if it does result from time to time.

How Can Journaling Help with All of This?

The starting place for reconnecting to purpose and becoming unstuck is listening to your wise self. And how better to do that than in an ongoing journaling practice? Stuckness comes and goes, and it lands more lightly and leaves more quickly when you have a steady journaling practice in hand. The Becoming Unstuck Journal is a practice and a process, not a product or an object.

One of my favorite things about regular private writing in a Becoming Unstuck Journal is its open-endedness. In the pages of a blank book, I write, often before the words have reached my conscious awareness. It's as though my writing hand connects directly with a source deep within (or beyond) my regular self. When I'm journaling, I'm not pre-writing the lines before they find expression on the paper. I write freely. In my journal, I can be myself no matter what. And "myself" turns out to have many voices. Discovering them, as they feel safe enough to show up, is a powerful and expansive process that provides a far-reaching remedy for creative blockage.

The following are a few of the benefits of sustaining a Becoming Unstuck Journal.

Support Creativity

We're not as constrained as we can believe we are. We can learn to gain access to more inner guidance. Whether you see that inner guidance as deriving from above/beyond, or from within, or as a mixture, is up to you.

I developed this belief from my own experience as a writer and musician and my work with authors, musicians, visual artists, designers, and others. Time and again, I observe that people can draw deep from some wellspring of creativity to their surprise and delight, even when they doubted it was possible. Your journal is a creative laboratory where, when you give yourself permission, you can amaze yourself and live to apply what you've discovered.

Park Rather than Juggle

Clearing your workspace to focus on one thing is a well-accepted tool to promote effectiveness and productivity. Similarly, you can clear your mind by committing to parking, not juggling, the multiple thoughts that keep you company. Stop keeping all those balls in the air. Set everything down in the secure space of your journal. Then you'll be free to focus on the one thing that is your priority at the moment. All the other balls and ideas you were juggling can be parked for now. You'll know where to find them.

Soften Perfectionism

Journals are wonderful antidotes to perfectionism. It's easy to misinterpret the purpose of perfectionism and to see it as something that's helpful, just perhaps a little overzealous. Not so fast. Brené Brown explains, "Many people think of perfectionism as striving to be your best, but it is not about self-improvement; it's about earning approval and acceptance."

The truth is effective journals tend to be messy and are, by their very nature, incomplete. Even if you use consistently gorgeous penmanship and perfectly spaced lines (I don't), a lively journal provides a winning argument against the rigidity of perfectionism. Those insights and fanciful notions and moments of inspired brilliance just would not have happened if you'd been monitoring or perfecting yourself before committing your words to paper. Once you acknowledge and experience the benefits of an open-ended journal, you'll be better prepared to stick up for the same welcoming approach when perfectionism tries to sideline your creativity elsewhere with unnecessary rules, judgments, and critiques.

Welcome the Problem-Solvers

When you allow yourself free rein in your journal, you invite sources of wisdom that are not accustomed to being heard. It can take a while to feel this out and even longer to begin to trust the process, so be gentle with yourself. Allow your hand to keep writing, even when you're not sure what the words are going to say. Make the problem-solvers and quiet inner voices feel welcome. Over time, this becomes easier. The rewards are powerful and mind-expanding.

Celebrate Your Wins

Your journal provides a nurturing environment where you can overcome your innate negativity bias. We all have it, hardwired in a primitive, pre-human part of our brain. It operates from fear, which alerts us to threats, to help us survive against attack. It can't be dismissed. However, if we try, we can rebalance our awareness to include positive things that also show up in our day, week, month, and year. We don't have a hardwired brain function for this, which means it takes intentional work. Each time you celebrate a win, large or small, you help your nervous system remember and value the joys, connections, and successes you've experienced. Make a routine of this, and let yourself celebrate in your journal. As an added benefit, you can strengthen your positive memories each time you revisit the pages.

Embrace Slowness

Once you get in the habit of this kind of becoming unstuck journaling, you understand that things happen in their own time. You come to know that some questions are not readily answered. By using your journal, you'll be able to unpack a troubling situation and, bit by bit, resolve the underlying concerns. You'll also allow rapid insights to show up and feel welcome. You'll remain open to the rhythms of your journaling process and let them play out.

Over the years, I have opened the pages of my blank books to welcome interviews with various interior parts of myself, inspirations, explorations of my emotions, ruminations on everything from politics to relationships, and reflections about my clients and our work together. My journals also contain free-writing, drafts for creative projects, notes from phone calls with friends, points to remember from webinars, podcasts, and books, brain dumps of things I want to do, doodles, names of books to read, websites to visit, artists to check out, movies to see, food to cook, community organizations to explore, places to go, reminders, and lots of marginalia.

When you cultivate a Becoming Unstuck Journal, you are the teacher and the student, the listened-to and the listener. You're open to the adventure that unfolds within the pages of a blank book and better prepared when fear tries to unnerve you on your quest to be and remain someone worth listening to.

Try This

Here are some ways to approach your Becoming Unstuck Journal:

- **Write Grumpy:** In a crabby mood? Habituate yourself to reach for your journal anyway. Even if it's only a few minutes of writing, you'll give yourself a gift, if not now, later when you revisit the words you wrote on that grumpy day.
- **If I Already Knew How:** When you're feeling stumped, ask yourself: "If I already knew how to take the next step/solve this problem, what would I do?" It's amazing how often a part of you who knows more than you can admit will step up when invited and tell you what you need.
- **Notice:** What specific things do I notice at this moment? Describe the small details: sounds, smells, noises, sights, textures, emotions, ideas, inspirations, thoughts, memories, etc.
- **Events:** What happened in the last twenty-four hours that I'm grateful for? What do I appreciate about those events, and what do they mean to me?
- **Let Go:** What can I let go of now? (Some burden, energy drain, wasteful behavior, inessential task, worry, etc.)
- **Listen to the Doubter:** Exiling a part of yourself, or an inner voice that you dislike hearing, can be futile and shortsighted. Instead of giving yourself a pep talk, try sitting down for a chat with the doubter. Write down the dialogue that ensues. Quite

often, that inner doubter is trying to help, perhaps based on out-of-date information or context, and open dialogue will reveal valuable insight.

- **Beginner's Mind:** Cast aside your expertise and instead approach a problem as if you knew nothing about it. This can give you the way in.

- **Is It Mine?:** When you feel burdened, stuck, depressed, despairing, anxious, or worried, ask yourself, as Robert Ohotto suggests, whether the feeling belongs to you. Often, the answer is a liberating no. Let that burden go. Re-center yourself on *your* purpose, your feelings, and your day.

- **Undelivered Communications:** In your journal, take Rick Hanson's advice and write out an entire conversation with the person, real or imagined, you're struggling with. Say all the unsaid things. Then write out the conversation again, with all the other person's responses. Pause and take in the result.

About the Author

A M Carley is a creative coach, author, teacher, and editor based in central Virginia, USA. Anne has been journaling since childhood and considers the practice a rich resource for creative people. Her nonfiction books, *FLOAT • Becoming Unstuck for Writers* and the forthcoming *CALM • Bold Creative Confidence*, encourage writers and other creative people to connect with and trust their inner guidance. One of the best ways to discover and follow that guidance, as her books, courses, and workshops encourage, is through a journaling practice. Her forthcoming *Becoming Unstuck Journal* workbook and its related online course provide an incubator environment where writers can expand their creative journaling practice. Visit annecarleycreative.com for information and to be notified about future publications and events.

CHAPTER 15

The Forest Journal

By Mary Ann Burrows

"Trees are poems that earth writes upon the sky.
We fell them down and turn them into paper,
that we may record our emptiness."

—Kahlil Gibran

Come now, to the sacred place. The trees are calling. Put down your busy world and step your sweet body into the magical woodland. Place one foot in front of the other and follow where your heart asks you to go. Stow everything away, become still, and allow your worried nerves to decompress.

We all need to find the time and space to exhale. The perfect writing spot is one where we can sit, observe, refocus, and reflect. This place is the forest. In the presence of trees, we are somehow able to crack open small pieces of our hearts, lift our moods, change our perceptions, and find all the answers. This brings us joy.

There is something spiritual about trees. After all, they have been here for thousands of years. Trees ground us and open us. Just looking at a tree makes us feel more rooted. We can sense that a tree sits as one with itself, in the energy of its presence. In the folklore of many cultures, trees are honored for their wisdom, worshipped and recognized as symbols of life and as holding sacred knowledge.

In a forest, trees are a community within themselves, each connected with the next through a complex root system. Trees work together, protect, and depend on one another while continuing to bring us beauty, food, and oxygen. Each tree values the next, taking only what it needs from the earth, nourishing and tending to its sick. The sounds, scents, sunlight, and fresh, clean air in a forest not only provide the ideal setting for us to connect harmoniously with ourselves but also bring us comfort and joy, making it the best location to sit and write.

To some, forests can feel overwhelming, bringing up feelings of fear and anxiety. One needs to feel both safe and comfortable enough to drop their guard so they can find the stillness needed to write. Going with a friend or in a group can help with this.

Every time we visit the forest, we melt away a little more of our barriers, allowing more access to our hearts. You will be amazed at what you begin to write when you are fully connected with yourself in the middle of a beautiful forest.

My Forest Story

I still remember the first time I played in a forest. Thinking back on it, I was too young to be in the woods without a parent. However, my little friend Susie and I spent most of our days frolicking through the trees behind her house on Little Mountain in the Fraser Valley.

As a child, I was fascinated with mysterious places where I could run wild. Next to the cemetery, the forest was my favorite place to play. I grew up in the '60s, where my bedtime stories included the likes of Little Red Riding Hood, Snow White, and Bambi. These cautionary tales warned of *unknown things that lurk in a dark forest,* but that didn't stop me from running freely through the trees without a care in the world.

Suzy and I spent hours searching for gnomes, our arms full of tiny handmade offerings and gifts for the forest fairies. Even as a young girl, I believed that offering a small bundle of flowers and foliage, handwritten notes, or a painted stone was my way of connecting, restoring balance, and saying thank you. Forest play brought meaning into my life and helped me create my own story to live by.

Back then, nature was my greatest teacher. I laughed as the pine trees threw their cones at my feet. I listened and learned as they held me in their branches and told me their storm stories. The forest taught me about birth, life, death, and regeneration.

Forest journaling as a grownup has brought me an even deeper understanding of my life and gifted me a peaceful kinship with myself and the flora of an ancient soul.

The Forest Journal

The most important thing to be aware of when writing outdoors is that *you are writing outdoors*. Things can happen when you are exposed to the elements, so be prepared. Bring a blanket, bug spray, etc. Consider forest journal writing as sacred, dedicating this time to love for yourself and love for the earth, and you will be given the greatest gifts.

Finding Your Stillness

Before we write in our forest journal, we need to be still. What is *stillness*, and why is it so important to achieve before we write in our journal?

Our stillness guides us into nothingness and brings us closer to our hearts. This is the place where our soul speaks to us. When we are still, we hear. The forest is the perfect place for this to happen. It is a beautiful, freeing moment when we finally discover our place of nothingness, the ultimate space from which to write.

Trees not only heighten our senses, they also simultaneously ground us. They give us a fresh new perspective and allow us to release, relax, and let go.

Wake Up Your Senses

Waking up your senses is a way to help you open up and increase your field of sensitivity and guide you to your stillness.

Preparation:

1. Find a quiet spot in the forest.
2. Sit or lie down on the earth.
3. Close your eyes.
4. Breathe.
5. Drop everything (old stories, expectations, and assumptions).
6. There is no right or wrong way to feel.
7. Become a part of the forest.
8. Hear the voices of the trees with your heart.
9. Feeling discomfort? Sit with it, allow it, observe it.
10. Even if you feel nothing, it is something.

An Exercise

- **Touch.** Bring your awareness to the gravity of your body. Feel your bones against the earth. Open up the sensation of your skin. Observe.
- **Taste.** Bring your awareness to the taste in your mouth. Stick your tongue out and feel the forest air. Breathe here. What do you taste?
- **Sight.** Bring your awareness to your eyes. What comes to your mind through closed eyes? What images do you see when you can't see? Allow what appears to appear. Breathe.
- **Smell.** Bring your awareness to your sense of smell. Breathe in the smells of the forest. Name the smells. What do you notice in your body? What images do these smells bring to your mind? What memories?
- **Sound.** Bring your awareness to your hearing. What sounds do you hear? Listen with your right ear. Listen with your left ear. How is your body reacting?

Now that all your senses are awake, slowly open your eyes and write in your forest journal.

FROM MY JOURNAL:

Sacred Oil

Soft, woodsy essence of rose, herbal accords with small notes of mulberry tree shade, wet with green earth and dusk.

Laurel leaves wrapped loosely with branches of fresh eucalyptus, muddy golden chanterelles and Lapsang tea, smells of Palo Santo and rainwater.

Sweet memories tease and toss up a buried dream of traveling to India.

Having Trouble Writing Today? Try This for Unblocking

- Look around you.
- Expand your peripheral vision, like opening the aperture on a camera.
- Without over-thinking, write down all the words that come to your mind. For example, from my journal:

April 4, 2018

Sky, lonely alien, unharmed, tall, primeval, ancestral, verdant, mature, cheerfully shaggy, faintly greening, beloved, conspicuous dead, healthy earth, damp moss.

This exercise may stir up many life memories, experiences, and feelings. Each word becomes a jumping-off point for a story in our journal. Pick one or two words that call to you and expand on them in your journal.

Signs and Symbols

There is a sign and a symbol in every moment, and the forest is full of them. Look around and find something that makes you feel joy, persistence, happiness, fear, or surrender. Here's an example from my journal:

June 18, 2020

A bumblebee

My creativity matters in the world.

By putting my own mind in the service of my Higher Self, I become limitlessly resourceful, creative, and beautiful.

I allow myself to be moved by all things, and to feel everything, fully. I am here to create, again and again.

Wondering

1. Look around the forest.
2. Find something that draws your curiosity.
3. Describe it in detail; wonder about it.
4. Ask yourself what it reminds you of. Here's an example from my journal:

June 7, 2018

I notice: A Maple Leaf: A burnt brown and orange, roughly toothed thin, dry leaf with five shallow lobes.

I wonder: I wonder why they call this a maple leaf, how tall do these trees grow? How would it feel to be an old maple leaf?

It reminds me of: A maple leaf reminds me of a time I spent with my father. He would spend hours raking up dead leaves in the fall at Grandma's house into a big pile. Later he would let me jump on them, scattering them everywhere. In that moment, I felt loved, adored and cherished by him.

End with Gratitude

I always like to end each visit with gratitude by bestowing a short blessing or prayer upon the forest, a small way of restoring balance and saying thank you.

A forest can provide a muse that helps us to see our life with fresh eyes. Trees call us in, begging us to stop and think. The forest is a place to pause, reboot, and reset. Free therapy.

Trees help wake up our senses and guide us toward the stillness we need to write from, leading us down new pathways of joy. I hope that you find yourself in a forest among the trees.

About the Author

Mary Ann Burrows is an artist, an author, and a nemophilist, living on the west coast of Canada. www.maryannburrows.com

CHAPTER 16

The Audio Journal

By Dwight McNair

"There is a sound for every thought. There is a sound for every feeling and emotion. There is a sound for every state of mind. There are sounds for every life circumstance or situation. There are sounds that express every human condition."

—Dwight McNair

When most people think of journaling, they think of writing by hand or using a computer to express their thoughts and feelings. For years, that was my primary method. I would sit down with pen in hand and write what was on my mind, whatever was bothersome, disturbing, inspiring, or exciting at the moment. And sometimes, my journaling would take me on a problem-solving journey, ending in what was often a solution or a sense of resolve.

But all of that changed for me about six or seven years ago. Over time, I realized that allowing myself to perceive and hear what was just below the surface enabled me to access and use a crucial yet untapped part of my intuition and creativity. I only had to take several deep breaths, calm myself down, clear my mental chatter and listen closely... to the silence. I discovered that listening to the silence enabled me to perceive, cull, extract, and give voice to my imagination.

For some time, I explored and studied the various states of mind we enter and leave just before waking and falling asleep. I began to observe how the content, contour, and quality of my experiences, imaginings, and perceptions during these periods were more original, fertile, and productive, no matter how elusive, ephemeral, and slippery they appeared. I instinctively knew that these states of consciousness were the wellspring of my creative process.

No matter how veiled or disguised, they existed under the cloak of seemingly chaotic and formless visual and aural chatter. It was hidden in plain sight and had eluded me during normal waking hours. Once aware of this resource, I was determined to extend and draw upon these moments, recreate and capture them, and mine them for future work and development. Thus, the sound-making journal and the process of journaling through sound was born.

One morning while driving home, I turned the voice memos application of my iPhone on. I began to tap a beat on my chest and proceeded to spontaneously utter wordless, nonsensical sounds one after another in an unplanned and improvisational way. Little did I know that these sounds and this process would form the bases of my songwriting and compositional process. Something had shifted. After this experience, I was flooded with new insights and deeply gratified by this new approach to self-expression.

What Is Journaling through Sound?

I have always been fascinated by sound. As human beings, we are always interacting with sound. We make it, listen to it, and respond or react to it. It is like breathing to us. However, much of this interaction is unconscious and out of our awareness. But it shapes and informs our lives. The sounds we make serve three basic purposes:

1. to communicate with the universe,
2. to communicate with one another; and most importantly,
3. to communicate with ourselves.

Number 3 is the one we overlook, dismiss, and take for granted.

When we examine how we make sound(s) in our bodies, how sound feels as it vibrates in and through our physical being, and how listening to sound(s) affects our emotional, physical, and psychological states, its value to us cannot be overestimated. The unquestioned power of sound to the human experience becomes obvious as soon as we recognize the impact of how it is received, heard, and felt by the body, by how sound oscillates within the ears, generates impulses through the heart and the blood vessels, and is interpreted by the mind and transmitted by the spirit.

Let me introduce you to a different approach to expressing and capturing one's thoughts, feelings, hopes, dreams, and emotions and chronicling the happenings and events of one's life. Journaling through sound is making any audible sounds, vibrations, or noises that are a natural part of our sound-making vocabulary. These spontaneous utterances are perhaps a more natural and automatic way of communicating than the act of writing itself.

So, how do we organize these sound-making inclinations into meaningful experiences? As human beings, we grunt, sigh, murmur, yawn, moan, babble, talk gibberish, whisper, speak, and make all manner of noises. These expressions are a part of our being. Journaling through sound is the process of using your body and your voice to make sounds that express whatever you are thinking, feeling, or experiencing at the moment, then capturing those sounds contemporaneously on a recording device.

These sounds usually fall into one of three categories: 1) speaking/ dictating words, sentences, or ideas that you can write down; 2) any audible frequency—a hum, a moan, a groan, laughter, a hiss, a sigh, a grunt, etc., that spontaneously flows from your being; or 3) a combination of these.

Making wordless sounds is another way of expressing and interpreting our world. This perceiving, expressing, and interpreting often happens almost imperceptibly and seemingly at the same time. Why is this process important? What is the value of it? This process and these sounds are important and of value because they offer another view of what is happening inside us and reveal aspects of our beings that are not readily obvious or available but contain much meaning and insight into deeper parts of ourselves. People often have feelings, thoughts, and emotions that they have difficulty putting into words, but that convey their experiences. It is common to hear the phrase "I can't put it into words."

How to Journal Using Sound

- **Step 1:** Turn on your recording device. I use the voice memos application on my iPhone. But any recording application found on most smart phones or any recording device will do.
- **Step 2:** Begin your sound journal by making sounds. Start with random sounds. With whatever comes to mind.
- **Step 3:** Listen to what you've recorded. Spend some time interpreting and giving meaning to it. Write or record your interpretations.

Journaling through sound is a freeing, creative, and imaginative way to open yourself up to hidden parts of yourself and often reveals insights that otherwise might remain unavailable to your conscious mind.

Journaling through sound is likewise a playful, fun, and stress-reducing self-care practice that can be used to awaken the spirit, energize the body, deepen our understanding of self, and heal whatever ails you.

Give the following a try (you can find examples of each at www.soundcloud.com/dwightmcnair-audio journal):

Turn your recording device on before you starts! Remember not to judge your utterances.

- Play with and experiment with making all kinds of sounds. Begin with the vowel sounds (a, e, i, o, u), then vary their length or duration. Sustain or elongate each one. Repeat each sound. Make each one short, detached, or staccato. Change each one's rhythm and tempo or speed. Add an emotion like sorrow or joy. Include all the consonant sounds.

- Sigh, cry, laugh, moan, groan, grunt, huff, puff, shout, scream, holler, whisper, whimper, murmur, screech, mumble, whine, etc.
- Conjure up and give rise to your emotions. Example: feel remorse, guilt, or shame. Without thinking, make sounds with those feelings as the impetus or impulse.
- Use body percussion such as: snapping your fingers, clapping your hands, tapping your foot, or tapping on your chest; or use small percussion instruments like a hand drum, triangle, wooden block, claves, tambourine, maracas, or cabasa to express what you are feeling.

Some Sound-Making Journal Prompts

Make whatever sounds or noises you feel like making. Then use your words to interpret the sounds. Ask yourself questions like the following ones to help you express these feelings and sounds in words:

- How do I feel when I listen to these sounds?
- What do these sounds trigger in me?
- Do these sounds annoy me, embarrass me, excite me, motivate me, or stimulate me?
- Do these sounds reveal anything about me that I don't want the world to know?

Some Sound-Making Activities

To relieve stress or anxiety:

- "I am so mad I could scream!" You could scream out loud or scream in a pillow (if you don't want anyone to hear you).
- "I am so frustrated I could shout." Shout!
- "I am so upset I could holler." Holler!

To increase happiness and joy:

- Laugh using the following syllables:
  - › Hah Hah Hah Hah Hah
  - › Ho Ho Ho
  - › He He He
- "I am so happy I could sing." Hum or sing.
- Pretend you are six years old, playing on the playground. Make sounds you would make or hear in that environment.

Make sounds that increase a sense of peace, calmness, freedom, tranquility, harmony, bliss, and healing:

- Ah
- Ooh
- Om
- Aum
- Hmmm

Try This

Actionable Steps

Talk into your recording device. Speak as though you are writing, using words, nonsensical sounds, animal sounds, machine sounds, etc. Use these sounds in combination or focus on each category alone.

Spend time with the sounds you have created. Try just listening and reflecting on them, feeling them, being at one with them, and gaining new understandings of them and what they may mean. What do they reveal about you to you? Move with them. See where they take you and how they continue to help you know you. How do they assist you in better recognizing your needs and desires? This may all be new to you and more than a little strange, but enjoy and learn!

About the Author

Dwight McNair is a singer/songwriter, vocal clinician, creativity coach, and author of *A Singer's Prayer and Meditation: A Spiritual Guide for Inspiration and Hope.* He currently operates a music studio in the Washington, DC area and is recording a new album to be released soon. Contact him at dwightmcnair@aol.com or dwightmcnair@icloud.com.

CHAPTER 17

The Conflict Resolution Journal

By Linda Dobson

"In the midst of winter, I found there was, within me, an invincible summer. And that makes me happy. For it says that no matter how hard the world pushes against me, within me, there's something stronger— something better, pushing right back."

—Albert Camus

I am writing this chapter during the second year of a global pandemic, for many of us a time of unprecedented personal and professional upheaval. During change, whether a pandemic or other challenging life events such as sickness or divorce, we can find ourselves more reactive and susceptible to large and small conflicts.

Many of my clients report a 'brain freeze," finding themselves incapable of understanding the entire picture, not knowing how to respond to perceived "attacks" and feeling so emotionally charged that they feel frozen. I designed the Conflict Resolution Journal (CRJ) for just such challenging times. Its simple process helps you write into your conflict experience and ask important questions about yourself to create better, more productive resolutions.

Before we begin, let's take just a moment for a brief biology lesson on why we experience "brain freeze," then move on to learn how to "defrost" so that you can understand and proactively respond to conflict. It all starts in your brain, which houses the amygdala, two cell groups in charge of recognizing threats and keeping us safe. Usually, the amygdala is our friend. Unfortunately, in times of stress—pandemic, illness, economic threat, etc.—it can get a little overactive, exaggerating risks and making everyday challenges appear bigger or more threatening. Situations that would normally merit a raised eyebrow or shrug of the shoulders become damaging conflict events. The CRJ incorporates the best of brain science, mindfulness, and conflict coaching theory, ensuring that our brains perform optimally.

What Is CRJ?

CRJ springs out of my decades-long fascination with how to create comprehensive conflict resolutions. As a mediator and professional conflict coach, I help clients identify, understand, and create practical solutions to deal with their conflicts.

Conflict Resolution Journaling harnesses the power of journaling as a practical, therapeutic, and clarifying tool, using the writing process and coaching questions that help you move through conflict when you find yourself distraught, discouraged, or dismayed. If you are ready to find authentic, values-based solutions to the conflicts in your life, I trust you will find the Conflict Resolution Journal an effective tool.

The Process
CRJ is an invitation to go to the page and allow your words to illuminate the inner workings of your mind and heart. The following steps will help you get the most from your journaling.

Step 1: Breathe

All you need to do is think about your conflict, and the amygdala leaps into action, reliving emotions and thoughts attached to your conflict. Research suggests that breathing helps calm the amygdala response, allowing access to your logical, thoughtful brain. To initiate a calm state, breathe in for four counts (you can mentally or verbally count 1, 2, 3, 4) and out for six. Repeat until you can feel yourself decompressing (this may be a body response, like your shoulders loosening, or a mental response, like less harried thoughts).

Step 2: Select Your Journal

I like one with nice paper, and I like using my fountain pen. It is an act of self-nurturing to surround yourself with the nicest things that are available to you, but a stick and a mud puddle will work in a pinch.

Step 3: Ask a Values-Based Question

"What three 'value words' illustrate how I want to 'be' in this conflict?" Write two or three words that come to mind (e.g., openness? Honesty? Curiosity? Creativity?) at the top of the page. Don't worry about getting the language perfect; simply listen to the words that surface.

Step 4: Ask a Goal-Focused Question

"What do I want/need to understand about this conflict?" This question guides your exploration of the conflict and sets a positive intention for your journal. For example: "I want to know what to do with my conflict with Leslie." Write your goal statement beneath your value words.

Step 5: Write

How to begin your writing? All conflict is composed of thoughts, feelings, and behaviors, and we tend to focus on one of the three when encountering conflict. If you touch your emotions most easily, begin with a feeling prompt such as "I feel…" or "I am really sad." If you are more a "thinker" than "feeler," try beginning with "I think" or "I believe" when recording your thoughts. Perhaps you focus more on the behaviors that contributed to the dispute, and it will be easy for you to write down actions such as "When this happened..." or "I saw." Try to expand your understanding by including all three aspects of conflict, thoughts, feelings, and behaviors. The goal is to keep writing and recording your experiences as genuinely as possible.

Step 6: Become Your Own Conflict Coach

This is where CRJ becomes delightful, illuminating, and bold. As you write, metaphorically ascend to the 1,000-foot level, reviewing and reflecting on your written words . Without any judgments, become curious about your writing, almost like a detective trying to solve a puzzle. When you see a word that is unusual for you or strikes you as slightly out of context, stop and unpack your word choice. Some sample questions include, "What prompted me to use that particular word?" or "Oh, that word is interesting; what else do I need to understand about x?" Begin to simply notice the mental shifts as you observe your writing. What are the shifts in your emotions and thoughts? As you read, observe your body and breath and explore whatever evokes different feelings or thoughts.

Step 7: Take a Break

Stop, leave your journal, make a cup of tea, sip a coffee, walk around your home, or look at something that brings you joy. Return to your writing, paying attention to the "values" words at the top of your page. How are your insights reflective of your values? Is there anything more your heart wants to say? Your intelligence? Your body?

Step 8: Take Steps Forward

Based on your journaling, what avenues do you see for moving forward? You do not need to resolve everything—baby steps are great. What is one thing you can do to think differently about the situation? What is the one small action you can take to move toward resolution? Now, set a timeline, and write down the current date and time, followed by the date and time you will begin to act on your new inspiration.

Step 9: Acknowledge

Acknowledge the tremendous courage and integrity you demonstrated to be real with yourself about this conflict. Breathe into your heart, mind, and body, and sit for a moment with gratitude for yourself and for this exercise ("Thank you for guiding me on this journey toward finding a resolution").

Try This

During Step 6 of your exploration, when you are blending your subjective self (the words are all about *you*, after all) and your self-coaching question (stay curious and away from judgments), flag any words that are or evoke any of the following:

- **New or novel:** Ask, "What does that word mean to me?" or "That is a weird word—what is that talking to me about?"
- **Repetitive:** "I notice that I have said 'dismissed' quite a few times and am curious what that means for me. And what else? And what else?"
- **Evoke a stronger feeling or thought:** "Whoa. When I write the word 'spiteful,' I get indignant. What is that telling me?"
- **Evoke a sense of resistance:** "Hmm, I don't like that word. Let me explore what the resistance is."
- **Feel true but incomplete:** "I am writing that my thoughts are 'silly.' Perhaps they are 'silly,' but what else are they?"
- **Give you pause to consider, or even stop you in your tracks:** "I need to think more about this."
- **Surprise you:** "OMG! I hadn't thought of that before!"
- **"Land" in your body:** These words may resonate in your chest, abdomen, throat—I see the word 'harsh.' I can feel that in the pit of

my stomach. "What else do I need to understand about this word and how it affects me?"

- **Evoke an "aha" moment:** "Yes, I get it—I see something I haven't before!" What other tools can help you build your curiosity?
- **Separate the person from the problem.** Note what behaviors prompted the conflict and address the problematic behaviors.
- **Note that your goal may shift** as you learn more about the conflict (e.g., from "I want an apology" to "I want to clearly and succinctly let them know how their behavior impacted me").
- **Notice the "pivot points":** Where does your narrative begin to shift as you become more aware or informed? How do you welcome the new, emergent, and informed story as it emerges? How do you move from "victim" to "creator" of your experience toward resolution? (E.g., "This is all their fault" to "I see I have had a role to play in the event and the resolution," or "Nothing can be done" to "This is how I see moving forward.")

I want to acknowledge that the CRJ is neither a silver bullet nor an easy process. Working through conflict is hard. When we deal with tough feelings and thoughts, it feels like slowly peeling away a Band-Aid protecting our hearts.

Harder still is moving from a "blame game" victim stance to a "creator of my own life" stance. Yet, and this is surprising and somewhat amazing, as you use CRJ and put pen to paper, something close to miraculous happens. You notice (as I do) that you view your conflict with less judgment and more curiosity. As you write, your brain begins to "thaw," and answers to your questions prompt important new insights providing you with a deeper awareness of how to respond to those deeply ingrained, evolutionary-driven fight, flight, or freeze responses. You find a are stronger, clearer, and more confident you. I send you peace.

About the Author

Linda Dobson is a mediator, conflict resolution specialist, and leadership and conflict coach. She has taught resolution strategies for almost three decades in face-to-face and virtual spaces. She is the author of *Coach the Conflict*, due in 2022, has presented at conferences (Bangkok, Victoria, Vancouver), and taught peacekeeping in Uganda and conflict coaching at the University in Mumbai, India. She is a speaker, writer, and educator who loves her work! Linda divides her time between Vancouver and Salt Spring Island, BC, where she tends her weedy garden and meditates on the tides. She loves laughing, playing, and great conversation. Linda hopes you will contact her with questions or comments at: lindadobson1@gmail.com.

CHAPTER 18

The Compassionate Journal

By Ahava Shira

"Trust that your heart is made for this work."

—Christine Pountney

I'd been working on this chapter steadily, and, deadline approaching, it wasn't feeling done. Sitting at my desk, reading over what I'd written, I felt a tension in my gut, right at the center of my solar plexus, the place in my body where I usually register anxiety.

Sensing that I needed a break, I stood up from my desk and walked away, made myself some tea, then sat down on the floor of my studio and stared out the French door windows into the garden, where snow was falling quickly, in random patterns.

As I watched the snow, I noticed it speed up, slow down, and change direction. As I continued to sit, I felt a warmth flooding my body, my breath deepening, my gut feeling lighter and less constricted. Looking back outside, I noticed the snow was falling more gently, its frenetic energy tempered.

I could have sat there at the computer for another hour, ignoring my gut and my body's indication of stress. I have done that in the past. But writing this chapter on compassion had tuned me into the intention, and I couldn't tune it out.

Pausing had been an act of compassion: Taking some time to relax, sip tea, and pay attention to my experience in a new way.

Learning How to See with Words

Insight meditation teacher Sharon Salzberg says: "It is hard to look at our own problems, negativities, hatreds, fears, and to admit they are there. We tend to cut off these parts of ourselves, to push them away. But there is a way of learning how to see these things in ourselves." In my thirty-three years as a journal writer, I have learned many ways "to see these things" in myself.

I don't know when I started to call it compassion, what Salzberg describes as "the trembling or quivering of the heart in response to pain or suffering." When I was feeling sad or scared, confused or overwhelmed, giving voice to the thoughts and feelings soothed me. More than that, I found other voices besides the hurt, scared, or confused ones. Kind-hearted ones, caring ones.

Through creatively shaping words into poems, inventing multiple meanings through metaphor or making up characters with whom I had ongoing conversations, I could bring soft and tender attention toward these experiences of pain and difficulty. Sometimes a brief freefall of words would release the emotion. Others required a many-paged confession of the struggle to calm the heart and remind me I was on my own side, and that things would be okay.

Freefall

In the spring of 1987, a few weeks before heading out on a three-and-a-half-month European backpacking adventure, I bought a lined notebook covered in navy blue cloth. I was twenty years old that summer as I crisscrossed the continent solo. Connecting with people from around the world, I had my journal as my one constant companion.

On a sunny day in late June, while sitting on a bench in St. James Park in London and people-watching, I admitted to myself that I felt lonely when I saw couples together. In early August, hanging out with some friends from home at the Pink Palace Hotel on Greece's Corfu Island, I had another compassionate insight, acknowledging a jealousy tantrum I'd just thrown. Already in my first journal, I was creating a space for compassion. Holding myself open to experience my vulnerability, I gave voice to hurt, loneliness, and frustration.

Poetry

Five years later, compassion arose as an impulse to creatively play with language. Inspired by a workshop at a conference in Seattle I was attending on women, Judaism, and psychology, I penned in my journal:

shelter in the wilderness
some calm amidst the storm
rest my tired body
bruised from the strain
of too much remembering
and torn open
by the agony of the unknown

what comes next
a woman a jew a conscious self
I know no way to choose what's best

let me live inside a while
where the darkness
holds the key...

(November 1992)

Over the next fifteen years, I practiced compassion in journal after journal through writing poetry. Then, in 1998, I published a whole book of the poems. I chose the title *Womb: Weaving of My Being* because of the Hebrew word for compassion *rachamim*, whose root is *rechem*, meaning womb.

Character

Twenty years later, in the spring of 2007, a different kind of creative impulse emerged in the journal. I was studying toward my PhD in language and literacy education, exploring the nuances and complexities of my experience as a healthy relationships educator.

As part of my research, I wrote a series of conversations between myself and a character I called Miss Understanding. After graduating, I continued to have ongoing dialogues with her in my journal. I would put her name, Miss U (for short), then a colon, and then write *her* voice. Then Ahava, colon, and *my* voice. Back and forth I'd go. For example:

Miss U: How are you, dear Ahava? (She sounds like a favorite great aunt, her voice warm and friendly. I feel calm right away when I "hear" her "speak.")

Ahava: Hello, Miss U. It is so good to hear your voice.

U: That's beautiful to hear. I do care deeply for you.

A: And I love to receive your love. I haven't always been able to see myself this way, nor talk to myself like this. Sometimes I still don't, when unconscious patterns show up as voices that say: "You're not good enough" or "You can't succeed."

U: Oh, tender Ahava. I feel compassion for you and the suffering those voices cause. Those voices are not true.

A: Yes, intellectually I know that, but they are so habitual that it is hard to get past them sometimes. They feel so real.

U: Ouch, and they hurt, don't they? They lead you to feel bad about yourself.

A: They do. But then there's you. You always respond to me from a place of kindness and compassion. Your voice is soft and soothing, and you know that I am not "bad" or "wrong" or "less than." You know that I am enough, even when I am struggling to feel it.

U: Oh, darling Ahava, I am so glad to hear it! How wondrous that you have made me into someone who loves you dearly. Through me, you cast a spell of compassion for yourself.

A: Yes, Miss U, it is wondrous. Through the written conversation with you, I give myself the compassion I need.

Confession

On a sunny day last summer, as countries around the globe were coming to grips with the magnitude of the pandemic, I found a place to practice compassion in an online journal writing circle. Sitting on the deck of my studio, staring at a screen filled with little squares, each occupied by a woman sitting in her own home somewhere in the world, we all wrote to the prompt of kindness:

> "Kindness is how I am getting through these days of joy and uncertainty. Kindness toward everything difficult, some of it already here before the coronavirus. Kindness toward my husband as he wakes mid-sleep in excruciating discomfort and weaves in and out of the new reality he is facing during the day. Kindness as I put my worries aside as to how his tremoring arm will limit his self-care, if not now or very soon, then sometime in the future. Kindness for the vulnerability so close to the surface in a man so proud of his self-reliance, a man still cooking and shopping and cleaning, weeding and designing a house where we both can live.

> "Kindness, remembering what the woman we didn't know said to him, as we passed her by in the lodge at Hollyhock, over ten years ago: 'You have the kindest face I've ever seen.'

> "Kindness that we give each other and our souls, our bodies, however they may look and function. Twenty years we've been dancing this dance of kindness. Oh, how grateful for its lessons on the floor of our life together. Kindness, thank you for the dance."

I needed to acknowledge the magnitude of my heart's quivering for my husband. The journal provided that space.

Metaphor

Over the past year, as I continued to express compassion for our journey of building a house together as we navigate health challenges, the phrase "a door within adore" surfaced in the journal. I played with it in several entries. Here's one:

> A door within adore, and some windows. The owner of the house
> has chosen ovals, shaped to suit a face to look inside and out.
> The frame of weather and trouble, what every house endures.
> A stove for warmth, place to sit and contemplate creation, corners
> where spiders have their way with thread.
> Up top, a loft of light, airy. Nights for rest and rejuvenation.
> Humans endure, are hopeful. Tender.
>
> Up nights, airy light rests on a loft for hopeful rejuvenation.
> Endure nights, tender.
> A place to sit, stove to contemplate creation.
> Spiders for warmth. Threads have their way. Corners too!
> What every house, human trouble frames, shaped to suit the owners.
> Adore within a door, some windows.
> Chosen, ovals, inside weather. Faces.
> Endure, and out.
> Tender.

Epilogue

Compassion is a movement of the mind and heart. It's an expression of tender loving care and kindness in the face of suffering. And it's a practice, something that we must do over and over to get good at it.

Try This

Here are a few ways you can practice compassion in your journal:

- Write a letter to yourself, addressing your hurt and/or vulnerable parts. For example: "Dear, darling Ahava. I see that your body is hurting, and you are having a bad day. Be gentle with yourself now."
- Write a dialogue with the part of you who knows how to be compassionate. You may ask them questions such as:
  - What would be helpful right now?
  - What words do I need to hear?
  - What words would be comforting to me?

Then let the wise, caring part respond.

We all need a space to hold ourselves and our vulnerability. A space to witness "the trembling or quivering" of our hearts, "to see our pain and suffering," and practice kindness and tenderness. A space to soothe ourselves through challenging times.

This place is our compassionate journal. May we all find healing within the loving embrace of its pages.

About the Author

Co-author of *Writing Alone Together: Journalling in a Circle of Women for Creativity, Compassion and Connection* (2014), Ahava is also the author of a poetry book *Weaving of My Being* (1998), a spoken word CD *Love is Like This* (2010), and the forthcoming memoir *Messy*. Her poems and essays have appeared in *Living Artfully: Reflections from the Far West Coast*, *The Art of Poetic Inquiry*, and *A Heart of Wisdom: Life Writing as Empathetic Inquiry*. A mentor of writers and facilitator of workshops and retreats in Loving Inquiry, an arts-based contemplative practice which she developed through her PhD in language and literacy education from the University of British Columbia, Ahava lives and loves on Salt Spring Island in a tiny "heart house" built by her beloved husband.

CHAPTER 19

Contemplative Journaling

By Kimberly Wulfert

"You might think of 'contemplating' as placing a boundary
around your interpretations, attachments, and preconceptions,
while deliberately stepping into uncertainty for a time.
Or, more succinctly, as in a haiku by Mizuta Masahide,
'Barns burnt down, now I can see the moon.'"

Contemplative journaling combines meditating in silence and journaling immediately thereafter for one to ten minutes. It is nonjudgmental and non-striving. There is no inquiry or intention set beyond combining them in time and space in this sequence. This is a journey between your deep inherent wisdom and living consciously.

I began a meditation practice in 2008 and began journaling many decades before that. For most of that time, I turned to journaling when I had a purpose in mind. My thinking, rational, linear left brain predominated. In meditation, I let my creative, abstract, non-language, whole-picture right brain reign. I did this by focusing awareness on my physical sensations as I breathed instead of on my thoughts and words.

Over the course of a few years, I discovered that when I journaled for one to ten minutes post-meditation, the spaciousness in my mind brought unexpected insights, connections, and perspectives, both personal and beyond the known aspects of my life. I named this combination Contemplative Journaling.

Silent meditation invokes visceral imagery and heightened senses that also engage with journaling, more so than analytic and memory-dominant journaling does. The writing has an ethereal, abstract, or metaphoric quality and sometimes takes a poetic or rhythmic form. Journaling inside this momentary mindset is a space that lets another level of awareness move onto the page. It slows the mind's rush to conclusive interpretations. Once written, it can be absorbed over time and contemplation, evolving, and allowing more awareness to enter your consciousness.

There is no judgment in the writings; they meet you where you are to call you to go deeper. The content or context can be broader than your personal concerns. It might reflect books or movies known to you, current events, geo-political issues, pop culture, and spiritual perspectives. The theme arising is spontaneous—serving only to awaken your consciousness and sidestep the limits of your thinking and life experiences. For example, during one session, the words came out exactly this way.

Mother Earth I hear
you calling you need love
you need air, room to breathe
you need space
earthquakes are your message now
for us who don't yet
hold you dear to hear
your cries, sighs,
your fears and tears
your message to us
to stop
and notice you are withering and dry
from being parched by
our robbing you of all you
need to grow and flourish
to regenerate, reproduce, and resist
the pollution, stripping, and heat

So you shake and crack open
showing how hollow and fragile
you've grown
now that you lack
love, replenishment, and breathing room
you once had
before we took you for granted
not realizing the pain we cause
was making you so sad
to the point of starving
you to death.

This was February of 2011. There were news reports of an earthquake in New Zealand. Climate change was seldom discussed then. Being neither a poet nor an environmentalist, why would this come onto my page?

In my early rereadings, I connected only to the earthquake because I have experienced them, and I was surprised New Zealand had had one. Contemplation awakened my dormant sense of agency and responsibility to the earth's state in general. I adjusted my values and behavior to align as partners in her care.

Sometimes only salient words, rather than whole phrases or sentences, are expressed in Contemplative Journaling. I put these salient words into a list. Some remain as a list, while others become stanzas or paragraphs. I once wrote, "fearful/trapped/untrusting/scared/mad/hopeful/grateful," which summed up my feelings at that time. I realized I was stuck, focusing on only the difficult feelings. Cultivating hopefulness and gratitude helped me move forward with solutions that had found space to show up in my mind with that shift.

You may experience a repeating theme, symbol, or visual metaphor over a short period of time in your journaling. The need for realization or insight on a matter is accentuated until it is understood and internal or external action is taken. Consciousness raised is not enough; it can quickly return to where it was when the habits of your mind resume. Your habits of thought are powerful and invisible until you contemplate them.

Try This

Combining principles from psychological learning theory and Eastern concentration meditation, I developed a method for silent meditation I have taught to beginners for more than a decade.

Meditating is easier to learn when you train your brain to work with you rather than fight against you. The brain's main goal is to keep you from harm and aid in your survival. Each time you repeat the steps that follow, you inform your brain you are safe, you are preparing to meditate, and it can relax for twenty minutes. After a few weeks of daily practice, your mind is alert, and your body is relaxed by the end of a session, and you can move into the journaling as described below.

Timing

Meditate at the same time every time. This meditation wakes up your mind, so it is best done early, before midday. I recommend twenty-minute sessions. You can incrementally build up to that if needed.

Posture

Sit on the same chair or cushion in the same location every time. Keep your spine straight but comfortably so. You can support your back but laying down is not recommended because it signals sleep to your brain. Unless you have physical limitations, find a comfortable place to sit up. Have your chin forward and your neck straight. With your eyes closed or softly opened, keep them still, focused forward and up slightly above the midline for the entire time. This quickly becomes automatic and helps quiet mental stimulation within. Your attention, not your eyes, is on your breath or anchor point.

Environment

There is no music, mantras, or guidance beyond what you might say to yourself in the beginning as you relax your body. Privacy and earplugs help drown out distractions and sounds that are out of your control. Over time you will be able to meditate in such conditions. The goal is to make it as easy to train the brain as possible and positive experiences are its reward.

Internal distractions can occur if you are hungry, feeling rushed, or physically uncomfortable in any way. Adjust what you can to help you let go.

Meditating

To begin a meditation, sense or imagine a warm relaxing energy flow from the earth into the bottom of your feet. Slowly let this soothing energy move up to fill every part of your body, face, and head like water filling a vessel from the bottom up until you are free of noticeable physical tension. This can take five minutes when you are a beginner, but eventually, your body will relax quite quickly when you sit down to meditate at your usual time and place. The brain is a fast learner. Repetition is the reason, so use this to your advantage in every practice.

If paying attention to breathing causes anxiety, choose another body anchor or focus of attention, such as your fingertips gently touching together in your lap or the soles of your feet on the floor. Stay with one for the session so as not to stimulate your mind unnecessarily. Surf the body sensations arising from the anchor willingly and effortlessly, as if riding a wave.

When you notice your mind is lost in thinking gently let go of the thoughts and return your attention to the sensations of breathing or alternate anchor point. Attaching to thoughts may seem constant at first. This is a habit of your mind. Thoughts never stop, but you notice and attach to them far less after practicing concentration meditation for a while. Calm breathing for an extended period also lulls the thinking mind.

Transitioning to Journaling

After a sustained time, allow sounds to enter and expand your field of awareness. Gently open your eyes, keeping them soft as you move from the meditation to your paper nearby. Write down the words that come to mind at that moment. This is not a mindless activity, nor are you attached to your beliefs, desires, and opinions. It is like taking dictation rather than stream-of-consciousness writing, and it is brief. A deep wisdom takes form in the spaciousness of the stillness to connect with you and leave its energetic impression in writing, usually for one to ten minutes. This is Contemplative Journaling, a key to open a hidden door in the whole of you.

Next, slowly read what you have written to absorb its meaning as deeply as you can. There is nothing to fear here, nor is it the time to ask questions, analyze, judge, or think. Become a witness to the thoughts and sensations arising in you as you reread it several times.

The brain tends to push toward certainty in its pursuit of safety, choosing closure over uncertainty. Henry David Thoreau said, "Wisdom does not inspect but behold. We must look a long time before we can see." Beholding requires a period of uncertainty. When the meaning is not yet clear but feels significant, stay in flux, pondering it. The deeper meaning can take days or months to be understood. Behold the original writing further through rereading, accenting, punctuating in different places, and journaling about it with an open, curious mind.

When you become as free as possible from preconceptions, from attachments to a particular view, and from unquestioned beliefs, there will be less resistance obscuring and limiting what you can absorb. Let the words and thoughts play around in your psyche and open up to suggestions from your intuition. As time goes on, notice any new or changing patterns in your life. Document the changes in your journal.

Contemplative Journaling fosters spaciousness in your conscious mind from which a new point of understanding can emerge. Rather than trying to achieve this view while meditating, bathe in its effortless silence, clearing your body and mind. Journaling within the space that unfolds immediately after, instead of later when you summarize it from memory, will be an adventure worth taking.

About the Author

Kimberly Wulfert, PhD, is a California-licensed clinical psychologist with a mindfulness-based private practice, a coach for women over forty in transition, and a meditation teacher. For decades, she has incorporated journaling techniques into therapy and taught workshops, often combining journaling with meditation to spark the creative mind. When the 2020 pandemic set in, she started *Journal Breeze*, a creative virtual space for women to gather and make arty journals to write in. She is a contributing author in *Transformational Journaling for Coaches, Therapists and Clients, A Complete Guide to the Benefits of Personal Writing*, edited by Lynda Monk and Eric Maisel. To connect, she welcomes your questions through KimberlyWulfert.com and JournalBreeze.com.

CHAPTER 20

Journaling as an Instrument of Mindfulness

By Beth Jacobs

"Don't try to extend presence for longer and longer periods of time. Bodhisattvas instead work on being present in shorter and shorter periods of time."

—Reb Anderson, Zen Master at the No Abode Hermitage
(from *The Jewel Mirror Samadhi Project*, pg. 74)

Mindfulness is frequently misunderstood. Most people have a sense that it would be beneficial to be more mindful, but that often translates into an impossible effort to control mind processes. Mindfulness is not concentration. Others seek mindfulness to blank out the mind and stop the processes of thought and reactivity. Mindfulness is not a bliss state. Mindfulness is a capacity to hold to, or to remember to return to, a dispassionate awareness in the midst of process. It is a neutral, observational skill that can be developed. As Reb Anderson notes above, the skill seeks to refine awareness, not grasp it.

I remember when I was first learning to meditate at a Zen center near my home, I ventured speaking to a young and kind-looking monk who sat with us on the black cushions facing the wall. I told him that I was struggling because my mind was "unruly," and I awaited his instructions on stopping that roiling mess I was beginning to perceive. "Join the club," he said. I was disappointed but had received my first lesson in mindfulness. It was great progress that I had begun to see what was going on and not just continued chasing thought after thought.

Mindfulness was first systematized as a therapeutic and spiritual concept by the early Buddhists, about 400 BCE. Contrary to their reputation, the early Buddhists were extremely rigorous and structured about both training mindfulness and using the skill to live a better life with less human suffering. The major teaching on the topic is *The Satipatthana Sutra*, or The Foundations of Mindfulness. This sutra is about twenty pages long, with thousands of pages of commentary on it.

The Satipatthana Sutra lays out basic areas, methods, and then objects of focus for training mindfulness. It is very specific, almost like a manual. By even listing these factors, awareness builds by stepping back and considering exactly what and how we are observing. Before reading such a list, you might stop and think about the four basic areas of your own human experience that you would use as categories for observation. The four basic areas of mindfulness observation in the sutra are body, feelings, mind states, and phenomena.

The methods of observing include watching experience from both inside and outside; watching experience arise and dissipate; watching the degree of mindfulness, not getting too superficial nor too caught up in it; and watching independently, not trying to manipulate what is seen.

These instructions help awareness evolve into insight. By watching from both inside and outside, we manipulate perspective, which reminds us of how important perspective itself is in influencing how the mind works. By watching mental activities come and go, we automatically experience the truth of impermanence, and that is a basic useful human realization. Understanding that all things change helps us face loss and waste less energy by clinging, a basic tenet of Buddhist teaching. By modulating the level of mindfulness, we remember to put the skill into the context of usefulness. Quick gliding over experience doesn't help us develop wisdom. Complete absorption doesn't help us function. Finally, the last instruction is the crucial reminder not to judge and react but to observe. We are trying to notice what happens without adding to it from our own associations and inclinations.

The sutra then continues with forty objects of meditation practiced in each of these areas and with each of these methods, which amounts to a well-developed capacity to observe through all types of activities. The point of mindfulness training is emphasized in the sutra also. The skill is not an end but a vehicle to insight. When we can see what is happening from many perspectives without adding our intentions, we can understand plain reality with wisdom. This makes us more accepting, more likely to be fluid and generous in our responses. That is why Reb Anderson refers to us as Bodhisattvas learning presence or mindfulness. Our acuity is meant to support our compassion in living.

Fortunately, mindfulness development doesn't require extensive training. There are shorter methods, and many meditative techniques are available in books, online, and training centers. But there also aren't quick shortcuts to developing any mental skill. Mindfulness requires repetition, intent, and a neutral type of reception. These are also part of a journaling practice, which is why journaling tends to link almost automatically with mindfulness.

By developing any ritual of personal writing, we build skills of observation and notice variations within the structure that repeats. We also write with the intent to let experience flow without judgment, and the neutral paper or screen, absent of audience, allows us exactly that observational space. We are one step removed and deep in the process at the same time.

Journal writing and mindfulness training have a natural synergy. The more we write, the more strength arises in our base of awareness. The more we value and work on our capacity to observe, the richer and more moving our writing tends to become. Our writing has a way of slowing down thought and making it more whole. Even if we carefully think something through, it is easy to go into fragments or vagaries that writing won't allow. At the same time, when we lay down those thoughts and feelings, we see they are just that, thoughts and feelings that persist in their time and circumstances, and not aspects of ourselves that we need to preserve and hold to in a rigid manner. We also develop a judgment-free zone in our journals. The freedom of writing for only ourselves and not for a purpose or an outside reader is vital. This is the core definition of journaling. Writing for yourself is mindfulness building.

There are specific ways to work with the journaling process that take the mindfulness building even further or develop more specific skills within mindfulness. Again, by considering the intersection of mindfulness and journaling, we notice a slight change in the practice, an extra layer of noticing, simply because we acknowledge it can be there.

Try This

Here are some more techniques for purposefully developing mindfulness skills within your journaling process:

1. **Ask yourself questions in your journal.** That simple reminder builds mindfulness as there is always insight available for the digging. If you are stuck, begin with *What am I experiencing right now?* You might add the traditional mindfulness categories: in body, feelings, mind states, and general phenomena, including things like weather, the season, current events, interpersonal dynamics, etc. Then it always helps insight to add the somewhat jarring question: *What am I avoiding right now?*

2. **Try to catch bare perception in your journal.** This isn't easy, but close your eyes, take three deep breaths, then open them, and try to notice the first edge of perception you take in. It may be the line of a chair, a color, the air temperature, or a sound, but try to notice how perception starts in fragments. Then make a thought about your perception. Form some language like *I see this blue curve* or *those clock ticks are making me crazy* or *ouch, my back hurts.* Hold the thought

in your mind and then simply repeat it. Repeat it. Now write it down. Then, write what you think about your thought. Notice how far you've come from your original moment of perception. This exercise breaks down what happens millions of times a day automatically in our minds and helps us see how much we typically add to sensory experience.

3. **Switch up your mind.** In this exercise, try four two-minute free writes on the basic topic of your momentary experience right now. First, just write. For the second one, become visually focused and watch yourself write. For two minutes, write while watching the letters emerging from the pen tip or keyboard. For the next two minutes, listen to your writing. Distinctly but silently say the words in your mind as they appear in front of you. Then focus on your breathing for a few minutes, feeling at least three deep inhalations and exhalations deep in your abdomen. Then try to write for two minutes while maintaining breath awareness in that simple way. This exercise helps you see how techniques of focus alter mind experience and written production.

4. **Catch your thoughts.** In this exercise, you don't try to write coherently, but you try to catch thoughts, impressions, sensations, or memories that arise spontaneously as you try to stay focused on breathing. Start in the same way as the last exercise by focusing on abdominal breathing for a few minutes. Try to see the space of mind as objects of mind arise, and then try to jot them down in a few words. Note what arises against the background of breath focus. You might end up with a list like sadness, quiet in ears, the kids, too much to do, gray paint, stiff shoulder, sadness, stiff shoulder. You might also end up with an idea for a poem.

In whatever ways that you purposefully play with mindfulness ideas, you can know that mindfulness is there for the asking. Ultimately, mindfulness is less about working than about dropping and releasing, less technique and more acceptance.

About the Author

Beth Jacobs, PhD, is a writer, clinical psychologist in private practice, and transmitted lay teacher in the Soto Zen Buddhist lineage. She is the author of *Long Shadows of Practice, A Buddhist Journal, The Original Buddhist Psychology, Paper Sky,* and *Writing for Emotional Balance.* She facilitates expressive writing groups for children, teenagers, and grandparents. For further information, please see BethJacobsBooks.com.

CHAPTER 21

Journaling Your Transitions

By Leia Francisco

"Writing about transitions brings a wisdom
beyond just thinking and talking about them."

—Transition journal of Leia Francisco, August 4, 2008

With your first breath, you begin a life of transition. You live in the
continual ebb and flow of these interruptions. Significant transitions
transform how you see yourself, a particular situation, or life itself. Even
the most challenging transition offers you a new chapter, a new wisdom.

You have already lived life-altering transitions, and you may be in a
transition as you read this. Maybe you are facing a change in your family
(e.g., grandparenting, the empty nest, divorce, or loss of a loved one).
Maybe you have a new job or career, or maybe you unexpectedly lost a
job. And a difficult change in your health may point to a new direction in
your life.

Every transition interrupts your life, often unexpectedly. A transition
is how you respond to a change or event, how you feel, think, and act.
These events seldom come in single file but often as a cluster of changes.
I call these "pinging transitions" because each transition bounces off the
others. Each requires time and energy.

Here is a typical example. "Emily" came to me for coaching,
overwhelmed by transitions. Late in life, she found her marriage was

falling apart, and at the same time, she lost her job as a sales manager. At the same time, her daughter moved back home due to her own job loss. How, Emily wondered, could she deal with all of this?

As it is for all of us, the key to Emily's navigating transitions was first understanding how transitions work. They consist of three fluid, overlapping phases: letting go, moving through the in-between, and creating the new role or situation—the new way.

Think back to your past transitions and the push and pull of each phase. As a young adult leaving home, you may have taken a job or pursued more education, but the process of being an adult pulled you between your old life and carving out your independence. When the economy takes a dive, people may lose a job or need to find a different type of work, which calls for letting go and moving from the old work to future work. Every transition is unique to you. Only you can determine how long it will take and how intense your reaction will be. No one else can tell you what your transition is or is not.

Over the years of transition coaching, I've seen how journaling supports transition in ways that talking and thinking about transitions do not. Transition journal-keepers mention discovering more parts of their transition, more possibilities, and deeper personal power. My clients and students continually express how much writing helps them see things—and new possibilities—more clearly.

My transition journal began when I left Washington, DC, for Texas in 2007. My journal was a structure and a nonjudgmental vessel for my feelings. In the roller coaster of transition, I could record feelings, thoughts, images, dreams, and questions about transitioning to a new place and way of being. Over time, those reactions were distilled into themes for redefining my career and lifestyle. I ended that journal by saying that I could see how all of us, even in the harshest climate, are "meant to bloom again and again."

In a big transition, you try to figure out how to manage the messiness of transitions. You may feel anxious, hopeful, fatigued, and excited. Your inside world and outside world are out of sync. Journaling regularly helps you see things from a different perspective and capture details you may otherwise miss. And you do not need to be a writer. Just be you.

Journaling sets the stage for the new chapter and offers a record of your transitions and your strengths in each phase of the transition. Pick the best time and journaling format to meet your needs at the moment. Date each entry. If you can, keep your journal flow by writing on a regular basis.

Try This

1. Start by Letting Go

As you journal, you will want to know what you must leave behind, what no longer works for you—whether tangible or intangible. The military person returning to civilian life gives up a uniform and highly structured career and culture. A new widow may feel the loss of a partner, changes in her daily life, loneliness, and how she sees herself. Every change, even happy ones, affects us with loss. We grieve. Becoming a parent brings joy and releases parts of the old lifestyle. A promotion means recognition and more money but can also change work relationships and locations.

The emotional process of letting go does not take place all at once. If you did try to let go of everything at once, you would feel overwhelmed. As you journal about endings, your body and heart will tell you when you are ready for each ending. It is also empowering and comforting to journal about what you do *not* have to let go of, such as your values, friendships, dreams, skills, and passions.

As you go through your transition, you can reassess what needs to end or not. Only you, the transition traveler, can make that decision.

2. Meet the Messy In-Between

In your past transitions, you will recall that uneasy feeling of floating between the past and future, the old and the new, with boundaries and routines dissolving. A common expression of this phase is, "I am falling apart." It is as if the old structure has been dismantled, which it has. Journaling helps you identify the pieces and discover some new ones. This movement is sometimes called the "liminal" stage, the threshold, and it is a time of exploration and reintegration.

Here your journal is a strong ally, truth-teller, comforter, and creator. It's normal to feel a mixture of reactions: fear, anger, fatigue, confusion, but also excitement, curiosity, introspection, and hope. Here is where great transformation is also possible, as you may remember from legends and inspiring stories you've read. Are you a bit scared to get big and wild in your journal? Don't be. The old boundaries are gone, so you have a lot of space for play. Capture the possibilities and creative flights with your journal, even if they seem like fantasies now.

Take the whirling thoughts and shape them with your words. For tighter boundaries, try short writes or lists, and if you want to explore further, let your journal flow until you are spent. Whatever feels right.

3. Create the New Way

Rather than using the term "new normal," think about a *gradual* emotional acceptance of the new way, role, relationship, or situation. One example is moving to a new house or town, which is often a big transition in your life story. When you move to a new house, it takes a while to get used to the light switches and layout to do things without thinking about them. Likewise, you shape the new way over time.

At this point in the transition, you begin to see how things could work out, and you are looking forward more than backward, journaling your hoped-for outcomes.

Try setting small, doable steps to ease into the new chapter, like introducing yourself to new neighbors, taking a class, or, as part of making yourself healthier, taking a daily walk. Research shows that if you write down goals, you are much more likely to reach them. Your journal is ready for your goals.

You might choose three goals for the next week/month. And if you do not reach them, write about what would have made a difference in reaching those goals. Use your journal to adjust how you reach your goals.

Hold onto your transition journal, and after some time, read through it and underline phrases that hold special meaning or give you clues to the next chapter. You might also journal a couple of paragraphs about what you have discovered, the wisdom you will carry forward, and how you might celebrate your strengths in navigating your transition. One of my clients reviewed her transition journal and was delighted to see clues and synchronicities she had not recognized. She saw her determination, even in bleak moments, and she saw that her instincts were true. It was indeed time to leave her toxic job behind.

Journaling your transition is your history and a guide for the next transition. It is a permanent reminder that you are both the author and hero of your story.

Name the Change

A good way to start is by naming the change you are facing, just some way to refer to it simply, for example: Finding out Who I Am; Goodbye City Life; Living with Diabetes; or Finding Love at Eighty. You can rename your change as you go along. Along with the name, list some resources you will need for your transition, such as family, money, time, support, and faith. If you have several pinging transitions, focus first on the most important one. Naming the most important change will help you create a baseline for journaling and bring your other transitions into better alignment.

Letting Go

Journaling guides your letting go. You may be uncertain about what losses lie ahead. Try journaling a list of what you need to let go: the big elm tree in your backyard, your former coworkers, your tendency to take care of everyone, your hectic lifestyle? These two prompts are favorites with transition journal-keepers: What ending is my biggest challenge? What ending will be easiest? Reflect on what will make the ending easier for you.

In-Between

Transition journal-keepers have found these prompts particularly helpful:

- What am I feeling right now? (Good for noting the normal ups and downs of life)
- What are my supports (a reminder to call on those supports)?
- I have had some wild thoughts lately (getting out of the box)
- My body is telling me...

New Way

In writing about your new chapter, you begin to feel new energy. This is a good time to celebrate moving through your transition and imagine the outcomes you want.

Write a letter to yourself honoring the strengths and values that helped you get to this new chapter. And write about what you are grateful for and the people you want to thank for their help.

Write a "future story." What would you like to happen? It is one year from the date of your journal entry, and you are looking back at what you have experienced and accomplished. Describe what has happened.

Keeping a transition journal is a powerful self-awareness and self-help tool. I hope you'll start your own!

About the Author

Leia Francisco is a board-certified transition coach and author of *Writing the Wisdom of Transitions: A Guide for Transforming Life Changes.* She has taught transition courses for The Therapeutic Writing Institute, Journalversity, and the National Story Network and written numerous transition articles for newspapers and journals. She offers a certification program in transition writing based on her trademarked program Writing Through Transition.® You can reach Leia through www.leiafrancisco.com or email her at lfrancisco@stx.rr.com. Her Facebook page is https://www. facebook.com/writingthroughtransitions/.

CHAPTER 22

The Writing Body

By Emelie Hill Dittmer

"We are chunks of dense matter that need to be cracked open. Our errors and failings are chinks in the heart's armour through which our true colours can shine."

—Elizabeth Lesser

When you start writing, so does your body, and these undertones may not initially be easy to decipher, but the deeper we go into the writing process, the clearer the signals become. It is like throwing yourself into a river of memories, an unforgettable psychological and physical journey through one's own history.

As we start exploring ourselves through our journal, we feel like we are entering an unfamiliar forest. We can become lost, to then find a path that leads us home, toward ourselves. Gradually, as the journaling process deepens, we begin to see with greater clarity the emerging trails, patterns, and moods that represent certain periods, people, or incidents that become prominent or influential in our lives. This complex exploration of tuning in to past life chapters and memories awakens our bodies.

Physically, we carry experiences, feelings, thoughts, and events and thus an incredibly unique story. Journaling is an effective way to access repressed memories. We need to take a gentle approach with this, as what unfolds is often surprising. Also, it can sometimes be acutely painful, especially if difficult or forgotten parts of our life story are revealed through the journaling itself. Our most shameful and painful secrets are also deeply entwined within our infinitely many unspoken stories.

To meet and familiarize yourself with your history requires a deep, almost meditative concentration. Allowing your body's music and memories to resonate through the pen can be likened to wholehearted devotion. The inner journey of writing involves many stops or pauses along the way to ponder and reflect on our experiences. How will we react? How will we cope with this *writing the body* process? The extraction of memory is largely determined by our fears and expectations before, during, and after this type of writing process and by how we dare to face and address these memories.

It is common during extreme stress to repress our most painful memories and the same can happen during our writing time too. We are experts at forgetting painful memories to cope with life. There might be times when it feels emotionally necessary to turn off certain memories. This does not mean that we want to reduce or erase our emotions, we simply do not want them to dominate our everyday lives, so it becomes natural for us to take alternative routes rather than allow ourselves to go deeper.

When I began my inner writing journey, the theme of *transgenerational trauma* took form. I felt a huge need to explore my family's history and trauma legacy, as well as my experiences of being a third-generation survivor of the Holocaust. The violence and anger I had witnessed, and that my mother had been exposed to for decades by my father, I had observed as a child in a silent shadow of destruction. I longed to discover where his anger stemmed from and how it had affected me. The bullying in my home continued throughout my primary school years and this was when I became a victim. Questions arose as the years went by, one being especially significant: *How had my grandmother been as a mother?*

I decided to get acquainted with my deceased grandmother's past through journaling. I experimented with many writing styles, including prose, poems, letters, fragmentary texts, diary entries, lists, dialogues, flow writing, and questions. But also with genres, narrative perspectives, tempus, and asking her the questions I never dared to ask when she was alive.

My early notes lead me to write the following statement with a shaky hand:

My grandmother survives the Holocaust. She gives birth to her first child shortly after the end of the war. This child came to be my father. My story is about how the horrors of war affects three generations and thus becomes my healing writing process.

Earlier with my journaling, I had attempted to confront my own family's trauma unsuccessfully. Now images of my grandmother came to me most powerfully during a particular writing exercise based on a dialogue with a body part, where my hands became prominent. This writing prompt was a breakthrough for me and transformational as I began to connect many dots of new understanding.

Focusing on my hands led to my grandmother's hands; hers were crooked, wounded by the war and the years in concentration camps. As a child, I had gazed at them and wondered why they were so battered. So were my mother's. Was there a connection, and why?
It was not until she became seriously ill that I came closer to the truth. The images of these women kept returning to me, but this time they were clearer and more detailed. I wrote the following in my journal...

It took a long time before I understood that my grandmother had been imprisoned in a women's camp. Suddenly I understood where the shame stemmed from. That you carried in your luggage Grandma and which also became my lead-heavy weight bag. That is also reflected in my mother's eyes, the day after.

I was unprepared for the emotional storm this writing prompt would provoke in me and how my whole being would express this. Had I known this would happen, I probably would not have completed this writing journey, but today, I am grateful I gave myself permission to do this. I strongly believe that one's whole body is a writing tool, even if it's the fingers and hands that are working when the text is formed. The process led to new insights, healing, and wisdom, including the following captured in my journal:

> The body has so many layers and undergoes several deep shifts throughout this process, where I believe things happen at a cellular level. It is a battle between the mind and the body, our truth and those of others along with our interpretations that creates a false sense of safety. By carefully entering, exiting, and experimenting with narratives enables transformation. If we persevere as long as possible, then the writing will return unexpected gifts.

The more we write, the more we access our body's wisdom, and this allows us greater access to our memories in a way that helps us avoid overwhelming ourselves. The more specific sensory details we can retrieve, the more life our writing will have, and our physical bodies will feel lighter and brighter. This is revealed in my journal...

> Writing about my childhood was especially stressful and emotionally challenging. My way of coping was to alternate mine and my grandmother's voice during writing. At times I felt a raw and indescribable pain, I both trembled and thought I was about to lose my voice. What sustained me was an unexpected stubbornness. When writing from the body, it may be helpful to take a detour through another family member in order to reach the wounds in a gentle way.

During my healing writing journey, I adopted a new perspective toward my family trauma, and with it came a new and unexpected calm. With that also came a deeper understanding of my background and how I'd been affected, and how my father's destructive behavior, just like mine, had its roots in his legacy.

I wrote because I desperately wanted to find the reasoning behind my family members' actions. Now I had a clearer picture, but at the same time, I realized that we can never map everything and that the most unexpected details appear when we start digging. By going to where it stings the most, I found unexpected courage, could recognize patterns, and drew parallels with unexpected clarity. It presented me with a new direction, but most importantly, it connected me to my body and encouraged me to trust its wisdom.

It is not a foregone conclusion that writing itself will lead somewhere, but rather the process contributes to shifts and vibrations undergoing transformations.

Try This

If you plan to write about traumatic events or more complex memories, remember to go gradually and gently. The following order is recommended:

1. Carefully limit your writing time. Start with shorter sessions of up to twenty minutes, increasing as you progress.
2. Ask yourself: Is there an alternative door you could open to discovering new information about the event, the people involved, or yourself? Experiment with perspective and writing style, genre, tempus, and even language. Healing writing can encompass different forms and ways of using language and can freely express and embrace what your body needs to say.
3. If you notice that your body reacts strongly to your writing, take a break and give yourself the space to rest, process, and shift your focus.
4. At the end of each writing session, ask yourself questions such as: How do I feel? What surprised me most about what came up in this session? Does my body feel any different from when I began writing, and why? Document your response.

5. Think about suitable ways to nurture your storytelling physical body. You have the right to feel safe and to give your body what it needs to feel good. For example, meditate, walk in the woods, practice yoga, and rest your body and soul in ways that suit you.

6. Try to vocalize your physical body and see where it takes you and your writing. Be curious and be open to the unexpected.

7. Try this exercise: Choose a body part, for example, your hand, that you would like to explore in your writing. Ask yourself: What has it been through? What has it created? What can you do with this body part or what does it enjoy? Try to write for ten minutes about your hand or hands. Give your body a voice and see where it takes you and your writing. Be curious. Be open to not knowing.

About the Author

Emelie Hill Dittmer is a writing pedagogue with a background in trauma-sensitive writing methods and journalism. In 2021, she published a Swedish book on healing writing.

Working as a course leader in the UK, Emelie first explored therapeutic writing in a group setting. Today she is more focused on teacher training in reflective writing techniques in her native Sweden.

She has run several programs in Writing for Healing Purposes, among these was the first of its kind in Sweden and was held at a state-run school for adult education, where she witnessed transformational journeys through the pen. Her personal story is her driving force. As a third-generation survivor of the holocaust, she has researched her family's history and trauma legacy in depth. Trans-generational trauma has been foundational in the development of Emelie's teaching style.

For more information about Emelie, visit www.emeliehdittmer.com and write to her at info@emeliehdittmer.com.

CHAPTER 23

Inner Critic Journaling

By Emma-Louise Elsey

"To find inner peace we must learn to love our inner
critic. Journaling is the perfect tool to help."

—Emma-Louise Elsey

Twenty years ago, I was perched on the sofa in my living room feeling edgy, weighed down, and tired. My first life coach was looking earnestly and encouragingly at me, and I clearly remember saying out loud for the first time that what I wanted *more than anything* was "inner peace."

I didn't know what "inner peace" was, but I *knew* I wanted it. And what commonly gets in the way of inner peace is our inner critic.

We all have *some* form of critic—whether we're aware of it or not.

Usually, we're aware of our critic because it's finding fault—judging us and others, our choices, and our actions. And when our critic is unmanaged or ignored, it can go rampant trying to get our attention. It can be abusive, judgmental, and relentless. It feels like being at war with ourselves.

But our critic has a positive intention: to be our conscience, guardian, and advisor. It both protects us and gives us that little extra push we need to try harder or do the "right thing."

Where Does the Inner Critic Come From?

Our inner critic dates back to childhood, when adults always knew best.

Our families, schools, and friendships all had rules (implicit and explicit) that we needed to follow to be liked, belong, and stay safe. We learned what pleased (and importantly, what upset) our primary caregivers so they'd continue to take care of us.

Your critic is simply the part of you that absorbed all the messages you received growing up and turned them into rules for you to follow.

And this explains why it can be so strong and forceful: the critic's goal is literally to *ensure our survival*.

But it gets complicated. While learning not to stick our fingers in an electrical outlet is helpful, many of the messages we received—even if intended to protect us—resulted from adult stress or misplaced fear.

Why We're in Conflict with Ourselves

Our young minds don't understand that sometimes adults are tired, afraid for us, or even just plain wrong.

When our mom said, "Don't get a big head," our shamed critic created a rule: from now on, keep your talents hidden. Or when a schoolteacher humiliated us for asking one too many questions, our critic decided: no more asking questions.

Our critics simply internalized these messages. And as we got older, these "rules" became habits.

Inner conflict begins as we grow up and become our own person with unique values, beliefs, and ways of doing things. We may no longer have to please or obey others to survive, but we're still carrying around the habitual thoughts, fears, and rules of our inner critic. It's this that creates our inner conflict.

And until you build a *new* relationship with your internalized critic, it will continue to assume it needs to protect you, as it did when you were a child.

So, Our Critic Is Really Just Trying to Keep Us Safe

Underneath it all, our critic is simply afraid. It will use any means, including bodily sensations, abusive language, and strong feelings like anger, rage, shame, and guilt, to manipulate you into following its rules and staying safe.

And that's why our inner critic gets in the way when we go after what we want in life, throwing up all sorts of obstacles. After all, what easier way to stay safe than by *avoiding* risk and change?

But it's impossible to go through life without change. And if we want to live full lives, we must go after what we want.

So what should we do when our critic makes this difficult for us?

Silencing Our Critic Doesn't Work

Many people think the best way to handle the critic is to silence and stuff it down, believing this will give us the inner peace we crave. There are many ways to do this (and I'm pretty sure I've tried all of them).

But until the critic feels *safe*, it's always going to try to protect you.

Yes, you may be able to push the critic underground—as I did. But while you may be able to ignore the critical voice, you can't stop the thoughts and accompanying feelings; if you've ever felt "unexplained" anxiety, you'll know what I mean.

I've learned that we don't want to shut down or get rid of our critics. We need to *tame* them. We need to get to know and build a relationship with them to trust us and relax.

Build a Relationship with Your Critic from a Place of Strength

Crucially, this means we must be *strong enough* that our critic feels safe, especially when we're trying new things or heading in new directions in our lives. It's at these times that we get things wrong and make mistakes, which is exactly what terrifies—and activates—our critic.

Your critic needs to believe you've "got this."

So... How Do We Do This?

I realized my inner critic was just a frightened child, stuck in the past, who'd turned to bullying and manipulation to stay safe. And I needed a way to stop it from bullying me *without* turning into a bully myself.

Simply being kind didn't work. My critic had decades of practice at being a super-scary tyrant. It knew exactly what to say to strike terror or shame into me, and when I was kind, it just shouted over me.

So this is where Fierce Kindness comes in. We need to be fiercely protective of our "selves" so our critic doesn't bully us. We also need to be kindly fierce with our critic, so it feels supported and understood—and won't resort to abusing us.

Importantly, it's not about silencing our critic; it's about changing how we *relate* to it.

Try This

Below are three exercises that use journaling to get you started on the path of befriending your inner critic.

As with any habit we want to change, it starts with awareness: recognizing *when* our critic is activated. Then we connect to our Fiercely

Kind Self. And finally, we listen and connect to our critics from that fiercely kind place.

These journaling techniques help you build a new relationship with your inner critic so that over time it becomes less intense, and you can enjoy life more and get closer to inner peace.

Exercise 1. Recognize When Your Inner Critic Is Active

Once you recognize the signs that your critic has been triggered, you can respond differently.

Notice your bodily sensations and feelings. Complete the following sentence stems in your journal, listing everything you can think of:

- I know my critic is active when I hear_____ (e.g., buzzing, ringing, things my critic regularly says, what I say or hear from others, my tone of voice, sounds getting fuzzy or more intense).
- I know my critic is active when I see _____ (e.g., people responding to me in a particular way, flashes of memory).
- I know my critic is active when I feel _____ (e.g., a sinking feeling in my stomach, butterflies, a weight on my chest, dry mouth, racing heart).
- I know my critic is active when I smell and/or taste_____ (e.g., something metallic, salty, burning, a strong cologne).

Exercise 2. Your Fiercely Kind, Wise, and Nurturing Self

In this visual journaling exercise, create a Fiercely Kind Self that your critic learns to trust, respect, and listen to. This self both stands up for you *and* helps the critic feel safe.

Step 1: Cut out images and words that "speak to you."

- What does a nurturing, wise, and strong you look like? Imagine someone kind, confident, unafraid of making mistakes, and fierce when they need to be.

- Ponder this as you flick through a variety of magazines, then cut out *anything* that matches this Fiercely Kind Self. Trust your intuition. Grab words and phrases that you think this self would use. Keep cutting out things until you have a pile of pictures and words to work with.

Step 2: Create Your Fiercely Kind, Wise, and Nurturing Self Vision Board.

- Arrange and stick the images into your journal or onto a blank piece of card in an arrangement that pleases you. Important: there is no "correct" way to do this—*whatever* you do is right.

Step 3: Review your completed Vision Board.

- Breathe deeply. Relax. What do you feel as you look at your vision board?
- Imagine *being* this version of you. Feel it.
- How would this self treat your inner critic?

Put your vision board somewhere you will see it often and use to it connect to your Fiercely Kind Self whenever you need to.

Exercise 3. Have a Conversation with Your Inner Critic

Now we befriend and validate our inner critic. Over time, with kindness, deep listening, and openness, these conversations will ultimately calm and reassure your critic. It will learn to trust you and relax so that you can enjoy inner peace and create the life you want.

Step 1: Connect with your Fiercely Kind Self.

- Take a few moments to feel into your Fiercely Kind Self. Calmly connect to this self, so that you feel compassionate but strong, knowing you won't be bullied or railroaded.

Step 2: Have a conversation with your critic, validating its concerns.

- Start by asking a question like, "Hi, inner critic; what are you worried about?"

- Now journal out the conversation naturally, swapping back and forth between your critic and your Fiercely Kind Self. Give your critic a full voice for all its concerns. Importantly, use your critic's words, even if that includes swearing, anger, insults, and meanness. It must be allowed to say whatever it thinks and feels.

- Be kind but firm. Do not allow it to bully you. The goal of your Fiercely Kind Self is to stay calm, *listen*, acknowledge, and *validate* your critic's fears and concerns.

- Continue your conversation until the critic has run out of steam.

Step 3: Bring the conversation to a close.

- To end the conversation, your Fiercely Kind Self should calmly summarize your critic's concerns and ensure it feels heard. Acknowledge anything helpful that you might act on. And lastly, thank your critic for caring so much about you.

Wrap-Up

Our critic is neither good nor bad, it just is—a habitual yet misguided way of thinking. If you'd like to go a little deeper, here are a few prompts to journal around:

- If your critic had a name, what would it be?
- Where and when in your life does your critic tend to crop up?
- What is your critic *most* afraid of?
- Where might your critic's thinking come from? Which specific people or experiences? Make a list.
- How relevant is this thinking today?
- How might your life improve if your critic felt loved and supported?

As we wrap up this chapter, what will you do with this knowledge? And when will you do it?

About the Author

Emma-Louise Elsey is a professional life coach, NLP practitioner, founder of The Coaching Tools Company, and most recently, Fierce Kindness. She began journaling in 2006 to manage her anxiety and a vicious inner critic, and although it was an awkward start, now she can't imagine a life without journaling.

Learn more about Fierce Kindness: a practice and philosophy providing inspiring and actionable personal development tools and resources rooted in courage and compassion at www.fiercekindness.com. *Change the world. Start with you!*

CHAPTER 24

From Journal to Memoir

By Eric Maisel

*"Each of us is a book waiting to be written;
and that book, if written, results in a person explained."*

—Thomas Cirignano

Memoir and autobiography have always been with us. Human beings desire to express themselves, and one natural way to express yourself is to tell your story.

This need is more pertinent and more poignant today as we face twin competing realities: it has never been easier to share information, and that we have never felt more like ciphers. More alone now, more lost in cyberspace, more disconnected from other human beings, up against a world that is melting down and tearing apart, we want to at least whisper our presence in writing. So memoir has exploded as a form.

If you have kept journals for many years, maybe even since childhood or adolescence, it might at first glance seem easy enough to mine those journals and relatively quickly create your memoir. After all, you have all that raw material and a record, even a daily record, of your whole life. All that material must be a blessing and better than its opposite, having no record, mustn't it? And yet, in my experience coaching writers for almost thirty years, I know that they do not typically experience possessing all that raw material as a pure blessing. Many writers find themselves paralyzed in the face of those boxes and shelves full of their journals. And it makes sense why they would feel that way.

Let's look at a couple of metaphoric analogies. Imagine that you had access to a huge university archive donated by a famous African American writer and artist, an archive that included her letters, notebooks, journals, diaries, sketchbooks, and all sorts of ephemera. Would you be all set? Not hardly. Despite that wealth of material, you would still have to decide not only what to include in your biography of her but, at a basic level, *what to write about.*

Are you writing primarily about her place in the Harlem Renaissance, and so bringing in lots of other writers, artists, and figures of that time into the narrative? How much additional research that would require! Or are you writing primarily about her relationship with her family? Are you writing primarily about her affairs with women and men? Are you writing primarily about the publication of her bestseller and its aftermath when the pressure to write a worthy sequel caused her to break down? *What are you writing about?*

The answer can't come from any of the following places. It can't come from landing on a particularly juicy anecdote: that would only be an anecdote, not a theme or a thread or the *reason* to write this biography. It can't come from a particularly dramatic moment (which in your mind's eye you see as a centerpiece of the movie you dream will be made from your biography). That moment may be vital for any prospective movie— but you are writing a biography, not a screenplay. Your decision about what you are *really writing about* can't come from any single bit that you stumble upon in that vast archive. Your decision must come from you *stepping to the side and deciding.*

You face the same pivotal question concerning your prospective memoir. At the beginning of the process, you will likely say to yourself, "Let me reread my journals and see what's there." But very quickly, confronted by all those pages and incidents, many mundane and some dramatic, you will likely find yourself asking yourself, "What exactly is the value or meaning of all of this?" and "What am I supposed to *do* with all this?"

Let's switch our analogy from a biographer trying to deal with a vast university archive to a museum curator curating a retrospective on a well-known artist. She knows that she has exactly nine rooms at her disposal and that the easiest way to curate the show is to go with "His early days," "His blue period," "His decade in Provence," "His last years," and so on. That would be easy enough, sensible enough, and maybe the right way to go. But how conventional! That curator may ultimately decide to proceed with a straight chronological presentation, but not before turning over in her mind the question, "Is there some *more interesting* way to present a life?"

Next consider a documentary filmmaker working on a film with an extraordinary amount of archival material of all sorts at his disposal: film clips, vintage photographs, letters, and so on. This being film, he knows that he can hop back and forth in time and jump all over the place: film viewers are accustomed to dealing with that rapid shifting. So, he has all the latitude in the world to follow that photo from 1940 with that bit of interview from 2020 with that bit of archival footage from 1984. The viewer will obediently follow. He can do anything he likes—but based on what rationale? Based on an in-the-moment intuition of what follows what and what goes with what? Or based on a script driven by a theme?

Biographer. Curator. Documentary filmmaker. They all have the same task: coming to decisions about what their biography, museum show, or film is *really about* or, if they never do land on that understanding, nevertheless putting together their biography, museum show, or film in some strong, sensible way, for instance chronologically. They may land on an inventive form, or they may have to settle for some standard form; and either case they will be confronted by an endless string of decisions.

What will go into this decision-making process as you face your mountain of journals? In addition to the intellectual task of deciding on the best frame, theme, or script for your memoir, in addition to the burden of sorting, shifting, choosing, and transcribing, you have the following four psychological tasks to address. Each is vitally important.

1. Are You Genuinely Willing to Reveal Yourself?

Many memoirists who believe that they are perfectly comfortable revealing their traumatic history, secret desires, shortcomings, failures, and warts aren't all that comfortable with any of that revealing. They honestly *want* to believe that they are because they don't want to be defeated in their aims by their fears and worries. But, while they *want* to feel comfortable, they may not be.

There is no more important issue for the would-be memoirist or the stalled memoirist to clarify since this is likely the main source of her blockage. This is also a tremendously important issue for the working memoirist, who may be managing to write but may be haunted by this issue and unconsciously censoring or "toning down" her memoir because she doesn't feel all that comfortable or safe revealing her truth.

If you have the intuition that this is an issue for you, how might you go about resolving it? There isn't an easy answer because we are talking about legitimate fears and worries that must be accounted for and not just suppressed. The starting place must be to have this hard conversation with yourself.

2. Are You Willing to Expose Others?

While you may be comfortable enough revealing your own history, secrets, and foibles, it is a completely separate matter whether you are willing to reveal what you know about your parents, grandparents, siblings, lovers, friends, bosses, or anyone else, even including someone as secondary to your story as your town's butcher, baker, or candlestick maker.

What might you be worried about? Embarrassing them. Humiliating them. Wronging them. Misrepresenting them. Upsetting them. Falling out with them. Being confronted by them. Even being sued by them. It's hard to make true progress on your memoir if you are stewing about these matters, if they remain unresolved, or if they remain a secret impediment to your progress.

What might your "right" answer be? It might be to carefully take each "character" in turn, see if certain ones worry you more than others, and then make some decisions based on that updated understanding. Or it might be to "put in everything" and then carefully decide which bits are too inflammatory, too revealing, or seem intuitively better left out. Whatever plan you adopt, the main point is that this issue must get cleared up. If you are half-unconsciously harboring the belief that it is too dangerous to write your memoir, you will not write it.

3. Can You Deal with the Inevitable and Continual Decision-Making Process?

Even after you've gotten clear about whether you're willing to be revealing, both about yourself and others, that doesn't mean that it will then be an easy matter to choose which incidents to put into your memoir, how many details to reveal, which themes to explore to the max, or what tone to adopt. Tons of decisions remain!

A writer writing her memoir goes ahead and makes these choices and decisions, confident not that these decisions are coming with any guarantees or that all of them will prove tenable but confident *that there is nothing else to do but to make one choice and one decision after another*. You must embrace with your whole being that there is nothing else to do but make decisions and only after the fact see if they were the right ones. Yes, you can certainly aid yourself by trying to make wise decisions right from the get-go. But as to whether they were wise, that you will only know much further along in the process.

4. Can You Deal with All Those Troubling Thoughts and Feelings?

Writing a memoir is provocative. It may well bring up troubling thoughts and painful feelings; it may trigger a flooding of difficult emotions, and, in the extreme, it can endanger your mental and emotional well-being. How could it be otherwise? You are likely writing your memoir in part to speak about the painful events in your life, an activity naturally causing you to remember them. This is dangerous territory.

Since you don't want to give up on writing your memoir because it brings up troubling thoughts and painful feelings (unless, of course, it does prove too difficult and dangerous an enterprise), you will need to think through what you mean to do when those troubling thoughts and painful feelings appear. You might want to read in the trauma literature, the post-traumatic disorder literature, or the addiction-recovery literature, as those are two places where a lot of thought has gone into how to heal the past and deal with the past in the present.

If you intend to write a memoir, your journals are a gold mine and a treasure trove. But they also come with shadows, demons, and difficulties. Your hope may be that you will simply sit down with your journals, read them, and mine them easily and efficiently. But it is rather more likely that there will be more to the process than that and that certain inevitable practical and psychological challenges will arise, stalling you and even pressuring you to put your memoir aside. Get ready for those challenges! If you intend to make your voice heard, you must meet those challenges. Your journals are a wonderful raw resource; then, the real work begins.

Try This

- Try to imagine dealing with your journals as a biographer might, as a museum curator might, and as a documentary filmmaker might.
- Try to answer the following four psychological questions:
  - › Are you willing to reveal and expose yourself?
  - › Are you willing to reveal and expose others?
  - › Can you deal with all that inevitable choosing and decision-making?
  - › Can you deal with the troubling thoughts and feelings that are bound to arise?
- See if you can come up with a solid, working answer to the question, "What is my memoir fundamentally about?"

- Given your thinking about the ideas in this chapter, how might you now approach mining your journals?

About the Author

Eric Maisel is the author of over fifty books. He writes the "Rethinking Mental Health" blog for *Psychology Today* (with 2.5 million views), blogs for Thrive Global, Fine Art America, and The Good Men Project, and has recently developed a contemporary philosophy of life called kirism, which he introduced in *Lighting the Way*. His many books include *The Power of Daily Practice*, *Coaching the Artist Within*, *The Van Gogh Blues*, and *The Future of Mental Health*. You can visit Dr. Maisel at www.ericmaisel.com and write him at ericmaisel@hotmail.com.

CHAPTER 25

Keeping the Fragmentary Journal

By Sheila Bender

"Driven by the forces of love, the fragments of the world seek each other so that the world may come to being."

—Pierre Teilhard de Chardin

When I edited the anthology *The Writer's Journal: 40 Contemporary Authors and Their Journals* in 1997, I sought journal excerpts by published writers and short essays on their journaling techniques. Among the most surprising were contributions from the poet Denise Levertov and the fiction writer Ron Carlson. They used their journals to record snippets of thought, observations, quotes, and witty phrases. It wasn't too long before I discovered Olivia Dresher's anthology *In Pieces*, a collection of fragmentary writings. Written in fragments, poems and lyric essays acquired mood and meaning.

I tried my hand at this technique and realized that collecting the details of my daily activities, observations, and thinking in short series provided a path for me to continue journaling on days when the well seemed to have gone dry. If I didn't know how to write about an experience, writing in fragments brought insight and discovery.

The fragments ultimately resonated beyond what I thought I had recorded. I came to see that they helped me find new meaning without struggling to do so. Writing fragments helped me realize I can write more than I know I have to write—writing short, writing deep, I call it.

I began devoting time to fragmentary writing exercises in the classes I taught to help others include fragmentary writing in their journals.

A journal itself may be considered fragmentary as each entry is a portion of the whole. But for the following exercises, I advise not thinking of the whole journal but of short entries built from "scraps." You may number or date them or put asterisks between them. You might give a collection of fragments a title and even subtitle the separate fragments in a collection if it pleases you.

Try This

Be Observant

Write about something that strikes you that you might not have thought to journal about. Here's an example:

Tuesday afternoon while working from home

I watch a young deer outside my study window chewing leaves from the Oregon grape I planted years ago because it is a native plant that served the Native Americans well with its berries. The deer is looking up at me and staring through the window now. I see the start of antlers, so a buck, of which there are fewer here than does. And back he goes to munching, now it seems on the fronds of sword ferns and on salal, another plant valuable to the first peoples here.

After you have written your short description of what struck you, write a description of what it makes you feel:

How I wish you were sitting beside me watching and communing with this deer. And back he goes, slowly now, into the ravine of cedar and fir trees.

Continue writing entries using this technique over one sitting or many, stamping each with the time and place you recorded your observation. After you have a batch of these, read through them and see what series title might help pinpoint the feeling the collection brings. If I kept looking out my window over several days at different times and wrote a short paragraph about the observation and a few sentences about how I felt after making the observation, I might call my collection of fragments or scraps "Love and My Window Frame Art."

Feel Free to Borrow from Other Forms

Employ the forms of voicemail messages, postcard messages, lists, and how-to instructions to help you find meaning beyond what you thought you would journal about.

1. Try making a list of customized outgoing voicemails for each day of the week. You could title the string of messages "In Brief: What I Want You to Know."

2. Write postcard messages to seven different people from your neighborhood, family, and friendship circle while sitting in different locations in your house, each on the same day but with different messages. Or try writing postcards to the same person on different days at different times. You will see how the content differs depending on the person you are writing to, where you are writing from, and the time of day you are writing.

If you want to create a title for the series of messages, try something like "Inviting You In" or "What I Say from Here."

For a new twist, imagine writing the messages from situations you wouldn't normally write: Postcard to my best friend while I wait at a broken traffic light. Postcard to my ex from the auditorium seat where I wait for the curtain to open on our daughter's play. Postcard to my mother as I wait at the checkout of her favorite store or the store I was not ever allowed to shop in.

3. Write lists:
   - 5 songs and what they make me remember when I hear them
   - 5 conversation openers I might whisper to a flower
   - 5 secrets I hold for others
   - 5 places I want to explore (they don't have to be exotic places, but of course they can be) and why
4. Imitate the way recipes are written and apply the form to something you don't usually see as a recipe. Needed ingredients are a fragment; instructions for preparing are a fragment; evaluating the outcome is a fragment:
   - Recipe for upsetting your teenager
   - Recipe for forgetting you were cooking something on the stove
   - Recipe for failing at fulfilling a promise you made to yourself or another
   - Recipe for lifting your spirits or bringing them down

Let Objects Do the Work

Notice five objects. Write down their names. Next, write a passage for each object, choosing from any topic in the following list, being sure to choose a different item from the list for each object:

- The most important memory you have associated with the object
- A fantasy you have when you look at the object
- Why you wish this object wasn't in your life or why you are pleased it is in your life
- If you were to name the object after a person, who would that be? Why?
- What does having this object make you miss?

Choose more objects if you want to and keep the writing going. Something important will evolve from the collection of fragments that evokes what is meaningful to you right now. When you have that body experience of "Ah, ha" or "Oh!" you might title the series of fragments using one of these exclamations.

Let Your Senses Guide You

How many times, watching someone do something, have you been suddenly overcome with strong feelings? List people you remember watching with deep feelings. You might want to stay away from anger, which usually covers up a more basic feeling such as sorrow or fear. And think small:

- When I saw you put your hands in the soapy dishwater
- When I saw your peanut butter cheek
- When I saw the ring that pierces your brown eyebrow
- When I saw you assembling the gas grill
- When I saw you raking leaves
- When I saw the unmatched socks you were wearing
- When I saw the elevator doors close in front of you
- When I saw you sit down at the edge of the bed

After the when clause, fill in what you remembered as you watched.

Then try using other senses, as well:

- When I heard you calling from the other room
- When I smelled the onions you were frying
- When I tasted the lemonade you forgot to put sugar in
- When I touched the petals of the rose you handed me

Again, after the when clauses, write the details that will bring the experience of the person you are thinking about to the page. You might write a title as simple as just "You."

Quote Yourself, Quote Others

Search for memorable quotes, sayings, or snippets of what others or you have said. You can search your journals for some. Pair them into two-line couplets and see what new meanings evolve.

Here is an example in which I grouped borrowed lines from different poems I wrote over the years, every line inspired by different people, times, and places:

Force is a clumsy power yet deftly we replace our children's wishes with our own.
We'll slay the alligators and claim our crowns from beside the velvet throne.

I sigh under the salty fog. Starlings fly like pieces of the brown earth crumbling.
Sometimes I remember years ago, the eagle we saw over the sand dunes
in blue sky.

I paint the canoe of your voice, let it take me again to the riverbank.
Sweet beads of sweat on our certain flesh.

Reading the couplets, I feel the experiences of my life even more deeply than when I wrote the original six poems. Fragmentary writing can do that.

Another way to accumulate writing from quotes, sayings, and snippets is to organize fortune cookie messages, snatches of song lyrics, quotes from teachers and parents, or snatches of dialogue you overhear. You can combine lines from all these sources into one "mixed media" fragmentary journal entry if you like. The two-line form guarantees one line will resonate against the other and encourage unexpected felt experience.

Use these exercises again and again, choosing different topics, people, occasions, and locations to write about. Invent ways of triggering and organizing fragments. Later, rereading the accumulation of fragments, you will feel amazed at the work they did even when you had no idea why you were creating them or how they would supply meaning, insight, and evocation. Your thoughts, experiences, yearnings, and understandings will come through in the fragments.

About the Author

Sheila Bender is the founder of Writingitreal.com. She is dedicated to helping people write from their personal experiences in journals, essays, poetry, and memoir. You can find out more about her, her books, and her classes at www.writingitreal.com.

CHAPTER 26

Journaling in the Third Person

By Lara Zielin

"Sometimes the scariest bridge to burn is the one between you and the person you thought you were."

—Tanya Markul, *The She Book*

For years, as a published author of romance and young-adult fiction, I was always asking, "What do my characters want? What are their motivations? What is a satisfying story for them?" But I had never considered the story of my own life. What was *my* motivation? What would make *me* happy?

That all changed when my publishing career imploded and my book contracts dried up. Within scant weeks of each other, both of my publishers decided that they no longer wanted to work with me.

This left me reeling. The identity of "published author" that I clung to so tightly evaporated almost overnight. I felt like a massive failure. I began drinking too much and pulling away from the people closest to me. I withdrew from my husband and friends. I was wounded and lost, wondering who I was anymore.

In this dark place, I knew I needed a way to change my story. Change your story, change your life, right? That's when I decided to play with the fiction-writing process, journaling, and the Hero's Journey. I wondered if writing about myself like one of the characters in my novels might help me heal.

For so long, I'd been asking, "What do my characters want?" and I finally began asking, "What does Lara want?" So, I decided to try and make myself the hero in my own life. I started a journal I unimaginatively titled *Lara's Life*, and I wrote about everything that would make the character of Lara feel joyful, happy, and fulfilled. I put her in wildly delightful situations—giving her trips, financial security, purpose, confidence, you name it.

While it was hard to imagine any good things that might happen to me *directly*, it was relatively easy to imagine the good things that could happen to Lara, the character.

It wasn't great prose by any stretch of the imagination, and, some days, all I could manage to write were some basic affirmations. But I discovered power in this process.

Within a year of writing this book, my life was markedly different, and, to my surprise, many of the things I had written about in my journal had come true. I realized I'd hit on a new method of journaling that didn't just rehash the past… it could shape the future.

When I set out to understand why this had worked, I discovered three primary reasons.

1. **First,** this type of writing exercise fuels pattern recognition. When you write down what you *want* to have happen to you, it helps you see more clearly the things holding you back. The tension is right there on the page for you in real life, the same as it would be for a character.

2. **Second,** writing ourselves as a character helps us understand our stories. Dr. James Pennebaker from the University of Texas has done research that shows how "storifying" experiences helps people approach what's happened to them more objectively. This can ultimately provide perspective on and understanding of experiences.

3. **Third,** we create more possibilities. According to researchers at Michigan State University and the University of Michigan, the third-person perspective helps people think about themselves as they would *others*. And often, it's easier to believe good things are more possible for others versus ourselves. (For example, think about how critically we sometimes speak to ourselves, whereas we'd never dream of speaking to someone else that way.) We can begin to believe in better outcomes when we think of ourselves like a friend, a colleague, or even a character.

However, the real power in this process is writing in the third person about what you want to have happen in your life and beginning to *feel* it. Engaging the positive emotions associated with your new story will resolve "future addiction," which can arise from writing endlessly about a future you so badly want but that feels out of reach.

Adding mindful meditation and visualization to this process can usher in the good feelings in your new story, bringing that reality into the here and now.

For example, my husband and I dream of wintering somewhere warm, and I'll often journal about the tropical Christmases we have, how we're outdoors in flip flops in January, and how magical this feels. After I am done writing, I set my notebook and pen aside, close my eyes, and feel the reality of this story. I imagine the bright blue sky, smell the salty ocean air, and feel the warm sand between my toes. I generate the happiness and peace I feel in this place and let that bliss wash over me.

This important part of the process collapses the distance between what I want to have happen in my new story and what I'm experiencing here and now. This "mind-body integration" is well documented by researchers, and the power of the mind to affect our physical body—and even our aura or energy, if you want to get woo about it—can significantly affect our levels of happiness, peace, and well-being.

Try This

First, get a notebook and grab a pen and prepare to go old school. Writing by hand is beneficial for the brain, helping us get creative and learn. It even lights up the brain in the same way meditation does.

Then, imagine your character (who is you) as if you were writing a book about them, and they are living their best life. They are the hero of your story! To start with, think about some of the best traits of your hero—for example, their compassion, their sense of humor, their love of writing, etc.

Write out as many of these amazing "hero" characteristics as you can. At a minimum, try for three to five. Then, begin to explore how this hero is feeling in their ideal story. Try to go deeper than "happy" and get as specific as you can about their emotions. What are they proud of? What brings them joy? How do they experience peace and freedom?

You can begin writing "[Your Name]'s dreams are coming true, and they feel..." and see what comes up. After you write about how your character feels, then begin to explore what they are *doing*. What does a typical day look like? What brave choices have they made to get here? You can begin writing "[Your Name] is so excited to able to..." and see what comes up.

Finally, what advice does this hero have for you in the here and now? Imagine your hero standing tall, their face radiant with adoration for you. "[Your Name], I love you so much, and this is what I want to tell you," they say. What wisdom do they share with you? What's important here is to keep it positive. Remember, your hero is awesome, and they're not here to chastise you or tell you how you're falling short. Their love and compassion for you takes center stage.

When you're done writing, set your pen and notebook aside. Close your eyes and take deep breaths. Picture each breath you take going into your heart and bringing in loving light. Allow that light to hold all the goodness inherent in your new story. Feel all the beautiful emotions available to you, letting your story begin in the here and now. Picture any walls around your heart crumbling and your heart expanding into new, beautiful possibilities.

About the Author

Lara Zielin is a published author, a coach, and the founder of Author Your Life. Through her simple, powerful journaling method, she teaches people how to stop playing small to create and live the life of their dreams. Her book *Author Your Life* cracked the top ten in its category on Amazon.com, and her articles have appeared on Medium.com, the Creative Penn, and Notes from the Universe. Lara lives in Michigan with her husband and dog, and her goal is to pretty much eat all the cheese. You can connect with her and learn more about how to author your own life at www. authoryourlifenow.com.

CHAPTER 27

Journaling in Community

By Mary Ann Moore

"Ceremony ... is a road to the true nature of our selves."

—Richard Wagamese

Wherever our ancestors lived, they gathered around a fire to tell their stories, honor the passing of each season, and celebrate rites of passage. Much later, people may have moved indoors to a kitchen table by a woodstove or to the back of a general store, where there may have been chairs set out for people to share their news. Women met around a quilting frame, sharing stories from their lives that wound their way through the threads and patterns of the fabric.

Today, we can apply the ancient wisdom of the circle to a modern application: gathering to create a sacred ceremony of journal writing, sharing and listening where each person is respected for their presence and contributions.

Over twenty years ago, when I affirmed to myself that writing was my wellness practice, I began offering women's writing circles in my Toronto living room. As a writer working in solitude, I had the sense of needing witnesses to support, encourage, and affirm what I was getting in touch with through journaling. And I wanted to share writing as a wellness practice.

When I think back to circles where I was honored, seen, and heard, I remember "consciousness-raising" circles of the 1970s, "self-help" circles, women's circles to honor the sabbats of the year, and circles that were part of goddess pilgrimages. A PeerSpirit Circle Practicum with Christina Baldwin and Ann Linnea, and the books they have written about the circle, have been a boon to the work I continue to do.

As I suggest for one's own journaling practice, a ceremony is key for the depth of experience. Part of that ceremony is the creation of a container to acknowledge the people in the circle and the stories they are writing and giving breath to. It's a way to create a sense of safety for the stories shared, lessen the anxiety, and honor the people and their stories.

As you are reading this, you may be the one to take the initiative to invite others to join you in a circle to journal together. Once you get started and following a few sessions, you can take turns being the facilitator of a circle where people can journal in community. You may have a theme in mind when you invite people together to explore journaling in community, such as gratitude or grieving the loss of life as we knew it.

When it is your turn to facilitate, at your home perhaps, arrange the chairs in a circle or as close to it as you can manage. You may choose to be at a spiritual or a community center or a private room in a library when you open the circle to the broader community.

Create a center for your circle with a few sacred objects, such as a candle, a bell to create an intentional beginning, an object that can act as a talking piece, a deck of divination cards if you like, an item that is sacred to you as the facilitator. I use a Turkish scarf in the center of the circles I offer in my living room, and I use a stone with a hand carved on it as a "talking piece." You can also add something to denote the season in your center, such as a spring flower, summer fruit, fall leaf, or winter branch.

Begin with a bell, the Tibetan ting-sha, for instance, or the sound of a rain stick to bring you all into the present moment. I suggest taking three deep breaths with thanks to Zen Buddhist monk Thich Nhat Hanh: one to let go, one to stay here, and one to surrender to what's next.

Read a poem to offer an intentional beginning for your journaling circle. Jane Hirshfield's "Da Capo" would be a good one as it is a term that means "from the beginning," and one of the poem's lines is "begin again the story of your life." Another suggestion is "Praying" by Mary Oliver with its line that says: "patch / a few words together and don't try / to make them elaborate."

To help create your circle's sacred container and to acknowledge each person in it, have a "talking piece" that you can pass from person to person. From the traditions of the First Nations, this is a way to acknowledge that you will be seen and heard, taking a turn to speak and be listened to with no interruptions or interactions with others.

As an introduction, when you have the talking piece, you can each say your name and where you are from. As facilitator, you could add what led you to gather others to journal together.

If you have time constraints, you could leave it at that, as people will get to know one another through the writing they share. If you choose, you could as facilitator, ask what drew each person to the circle. When a person is finished talking, they pass the "talking piece" to the next person or put it in the center for someone else to take.

What will you write about? The opening poem could give you a prompt to begin. I suggested a Mary Oliver poem, and if you have read her poetry, you'll know that many of them have questions such as "The Summer Day," which ends with, "Tell me, what is it you plan to do with your one wild and precious life?"

A question can act as a prompt or picking a card from a divination deck. One poem can offer several prompts such as "The World Ends Here," a poem by Joy Harjo, the poet laureate of the United States, or the words of a song such as "The Book of My Life" by Sting.

Take about fifteen to twenty minutes to write on each theme.

People can share if they'd like. It's important that everyone listen to the person speaking; this could be the first time they are reading something of their own to others.

When making comments following the reading, if any, say what words or phrases resonate with you. Echo back those words to the person reading their piece out loud. Say what you appreciate about the writing you've heard. When we pay attention to what resonates with us and give a response from that heart-felt place, we're offering reassurance and an honoring of one's voice. It will help to further the writer's confidence in continuing to explore and express their story.

This is not a time to recall, as listener, your own story, at least not out loud. It's time to listen to the person reading and reflect on what stood out for you in their story. It is not a time to exclaim, critique, or question but simply to be with the words you heard. There is great courage and vulnerability in giving voice to one's words, and it is a time to be tender with one another.

Perhaps there are some logistics to share, such as when and where you will meet again and who will facilitate.

Pass the "talking piece" again, at the close of your circle, so that people have an opportunity to share how they're feeling following the writing and sharing they have done. Read a poem to close, perhaps "Blessing" by John O'Donohue or "Blessing for a Writer" by Pat Schneider.

I have facilitated circles for teenagers, women in a First Nation's community, at a drop-in for people in the mental health community, and women in creative writing classes. I have attended poetry retreats where I value the connections I have to others by meeting in this way as we learn about one another through our writing and our deepest feelings. We're not looking at occupations, financial status, or any other sort of status.

Journaling in a circle where you have created a ceremony offers infinite possibilities as you are seen and heard by companions who witness your writing journey. I hope you will find this way of connecting to others in community an enriching one and that the support of others helps you deepen your story, and you come to value it even more.

At the end of the circles I facilitate, I say:

The circle is open but unbroken
merry meet and merry part
and merry meet again

Try This

- Make some notes about circles you have been part of before and what worked well about them.
- Think about who you may want to invite to a circle to journal together. These could be people you know before you "advertise" to the public. Begin to make a list.
- What objects will you put in the center of your circle?
- Have a look at your bookshelves for anthologies of poetry or other inspirational work that you could use as opening and closing readings and journaling prompts in your circle.
- Express any fears and concerns you have about your proposed journaling circle on paper, and take a deep breath.
- Begin with one other person to explore journaling together.

About the Author

Mary Ann Moore is a poet, writer, and writing mentor based in Nanaimo, British Columbia. She leads poetry workshops, women's writing circles called Writing Life, and offers a mentoring program called *Writing Home: A Whole Life Practice*. Mary Ann is a member of the Journal Council of the International Association for Journal Writing (IAJW). Through the IAJW, she offers a digital writing resource called *Writing to Map Your Spiritual Journey* and a journaling tool called *Your Own Tea House Practice*. Mary Ann's poetry, essays, book reviews, and author profiles have appeared in many journals and newspapers. Her book of poetry is *Fishing for Mermaids* (Leaf Press). Visit her website at www.maryannmoore.ca.

CHAPTER 28

Journaling in a Group: A Facilitator's Perspective

By Nancy Johnston

"Determined, the writer looks at a slip of blank paper
with hope that she will know what to do, that in quick
succession a string of sentences will begin to appear,
and these she will manage to rope into beauty and order."

—Maya Stein

A journal writing group can be a fulfilling experience for participants because it creates community through the shared writing process, helps individuals explore new ideas, and sustains their writing through group practice.

We might join a group because we share a love and excitement for expressive writing or journaling or sharing work with a supportive group. We find a place that stimulates new ideas through expressive writing prompts and carve some time for our creativity. Although many groups can grow spontaneously from friends or are an extension of a writing workshop, other writing and journaling groups are created deliberately by peer leaders and facilitators.

Leading and facilitating a writing group can also be a joy. In this chapter, I'd like to share my perspective as a writing teacher and co-facilitator for an expressive writing group for university staff who identify as women. My strategies include tips for keeping up your energy as a facilitator, collaborating with a peer group of writers, developing writing prompts, inspiring a positive group dynamic, and creating a safe writing environment.

The work of a facilitator and organizer can be time-consuming, but for me, it has always been fulfilling. Over the last five years as a co-founder and co-facilitator, I've welcomed dozens of new and returning women to the group, created numerous writing prompts for monthly sessions, shared community meals, and collaborated on organizing large campus events for International Women's Day. I've organized many workshops and events over the years, but my collaboration on the Women's Writing Circle has been the longest-running and most fulfilling of my career.

The idea for a writing circle began as a conversation between three women—Sarah King, Toni DeMello, and me—and grew to include my current co-facilitator, Shehna Javeed. Our group's aim was to offer expressive writing and journaling as support for the mutual mental health and wellness of women who work in our university community.

Our goals in our monthly group are to write for personal expression, create community connections, and build our resilience by writing about experiences, ideas, and emotions. To create this space as facilitators and participants, we have built on shared respect for each other and trust in the process. We encourage creative expression and minimize critique by holding a positive space for expression. We encourage participants to do two short, timed free-writes without self-censoring. Everyone is invited, but not required, to share something about the writing experience or to read from their writing.

The role of the facilitators is to make sure everyone is included and has an opportunity to share. As facilitators, we model the writing process but also actively participate as writers and as listeners. One of our regular members captured the positive energy of the group: "For someone that routinely feels somewhat of a misfit at work, this was different; it made me feel like I actually belonged (with many others expressing similar sentiments to my own)." Our members face time constraints at work, so we run our sessions during lunch hour and welcome everyone individually with social time in each session. For many, the group is a safe haven, where they can have time for more creativity in their lives.

When we decided to form a writing circle group and run monthly sessions, it was a leap of faith. Although collectively, we had years of experience running groups and workshops, we did not know if our goals would resonate with our community until we tried. I'd like to share some insights into the planning process behind our successful group. Once you decide to run a writing group or event, the next steps are often focused on how to make the group as cohesive and inclusive as possible.

Try This

Planning a Journal Writing Group

1. **Work with a partner or team.** Delegate or share pre-event organizing duties, such as creating posters or emailing reminders, and co-facilitate during your writing group. At an in-person or online event, co-facilitators or partners can support each other by sharing or alternating their roles. Avoid the problem of multi-tasking. Co-facilitators can decide to divide their attention between presenting a writing prompt, welcoming late-comers, and watching the clock.

2. **Think about inclusion when planning.** What size group will work best for the facilitators and the group? Do you have an accessible space or venue convenient for your community? If you're working with a community group or organization such as a library, ask about any barriers and supports in place. As organizers, you may want to discuss your goals for the group and how to share your objectives and format with your group.

In our women's writing circle sessions, we review our goals and format in each session. When we have newcomers to the group, we may ask a group member to review principles of confidentiality, positive feedback, and options in sharing. When you are planning an online group, it is especially important to share information on accessing your group session. Group members less familiar with online platforms may need help unmuting and participating. Options may be to open your session early for troubleshooting and sharing instructions.

3. **Create a welcoming space.** Participants thrive on writing in a group and remark that it is different than writing independently. However, new participants may be nervous or unsure of what to expect. A facilitator makes the space welcoming by letting the group get to know each other. We open our groups by socializing and by sharing food to create a feeling of comfort. Returning members may share their experience writing and encourage newcomers. Take time to greet each participant and introduce yourself. This is a positive ritual that also creates mutual trust.

4. **Collaborate with group members.** Invite your members to contribute their ideas for writing prompts and for ways of channeling their enthusiasm. Include participants in some planning when you are established. They may have practical experience and enjoy helping in outreach, running events, or even online troubleshooting.

Creating Journal Writing Prompts and Exercises

The following are ideas about creating prompts and delivering them. As an organizer or facilitator, you've put a lot of effort into creating a safe and welcoming space, introducing writing prompts and discussions, encouraging everyone to begin writing. You've done your part in setting a stage for the writing process. Not every prompt or exercise is going to work. Remember that most arrive wanting to write and to share in the creative process. Here are some ideas:

1. **Create new prompts or adapt them.** I think about my group's interests and current topics or events, like Black History Month or interests in newly published books. Avoid choosing prompts from a generic or master list as those can feel limiting to your participants. If you ask your group of writers to answer a question like, "What are your New Year's Resolutions?" many will reveal they don't keep them. Rather than have this approach shut down writing, try a more open-ended prompt. The writing advice and exercises offered by creative writers and coaches, such as Eric Maisel, Lynda Barry, and Natalie Goldberg, may be better sources because they offer prompts with more context about the writing process and motivation.

   Try to stay attentive to the mood of your group, whether they have interests in poetry or a desire for supportive or explorative work. I've introduced writing prompts that might reflect seasonal events or relate to issues related to their experience as women. One writer responded to a prompt to write about an important woman who was a storyteller in her life. She shared, "My aunties were story-keepers who only opened up when we worked side by side. They revealed secrets when doing the dishes."

2. **Think about how you'll introduce your exercises and prompts.** Give a brief preamble or personal story. Why is this topic exciting or topical for you? Read and reread the prompt for the group. Offer a sentence stem or a way to begin as an option for writers. Remind writers to free-write without stopping and without self-criticism.

3. **Open and close the space for each writing exercise.** Think of the opening of writing space as a kind of ritual. After reading and repeating your prompt, invite everyone to begin. Announce the length of time to write. If you are trying several prompts, start with a short one, perhaps try five to seven minutes, as a warm-up. Remind your group gently when the time is ending. Suggest that they finish their sentence or draw a line. Open the floor with a meditative breath and a pause.

4. **Make room for sharing without reading original writing.** Be patient. Rather than calling on specific people, consider inviting anyone to share their writing experience on this prompt. Someone may disclose that the prompt was difficult and appreciate discussing it. Others may say they continued and ended up somewhere surprising. Share a few lines of your writing on the prompt to encourage others to write.

5. **Be less ambitious with the number of prompts and exercises.** Freewriting is about generating ideas and moving your pen forward. You may be tempted to offer more fabulous exercises and prompts than can easily fit into the group time. This is important to consider if your group is sharing their writing and ideas. Try fewer prompts with your group. Trust the writing process.

About the Author

Nancy Johnston is a teacher, writing coach, writer, and textile artist living in Toronto. She co-founded the Women's Writing Circle in 2016 with her colleagues. She is an associate professor who teaches writing and disability studies at the University of Toronto Scarborough. Her passions are teaching writing and textile art for expressive and restorative play.

CHAPTER 29

Journaling with Children

By Nicolle Nattrass

"There can be no keener revelation of a society's soul
than the way in which it treats its children."

—Nelson Mandela, former president of South Africa

In this chapter, I'd like to explain how you can use journaling with the tender hearts in our lives, our children. I've used journaling to help my son and family recover from a traumatic car accident and in my work as an addiction counselor I take a trauma-informed approach that employs creative journaling as a key recovery tool to help children (age four and up) to process stress, anxiety, trauma. Let me explain.

Do you remember your first journal? I do. I still have it to this day and bring it with me when I give keynotes or workshops. My first journal was a five-year personal diary, blue vinyl with padlock, which came with the tiniest key. Each page was lined and crammed with my impressive cursive handwriting. Not all pages are full but as I look through that little blue diary, I am struck by this entry:

Today was awful, everyone thinks I am little and can't do anything.

A short but profound entry. It reminds me of how deeply children experience the world and how lightly we treat their experiences. My book *Just the Two of Us: A Soft Place for Tender Hearts to Land* documents much more than my professional experience using journaling as a counselor with clients. I came to discover and explore journaling with children after facing what no parent expects to face: witnessing the effects of trauma on their child.

In 2013, when our son was four years old, our family experienced a traumatic motor vehicle accident. Thankfully, he was not physically injured, save for a small cut and bruising from the straps on his car seat that had kept him safely in place. However, the emotional and mental impact was significantly life-changing, enough that there was no way we could ignore it or chalk it up as an unfortunate event best forgotten.

Despite well-meaning suggestions to "try not to talk about the car accident and that maybe he would forget about it in a couple of weeks," we could not and did not. He was sending out disturbing signals. For example, in his play, he was building towers in places where they were sure to be knocked down in passing or placing them near our front door. When they did fall over, the emotional distress he displayed was more than a normal response. I began paying closer attention, having been trained to notice signs and symptoms of PTSD when I worked as a frontline addiction counselor in residential treatment.

Concerned, I searched everywhere and did find some resources, including the National Child Trauma Network. I looked at their recommendations for services suitable for children and began to ask around in my community about what might help. As I researched the minimal help available, I realized, both as a parent and therapeutic counseling professional, that the resources were limited for helping children who were too young for talk therapy but needed support.

It was clear that the nearby resources were limited and not age-appropriate. I was not comfortable leaving my child alone in a therapy session with anyone at this time, as he was experiencing great separation anxiety. Many of the existing resources that could help him were far away in bigger cities, requiring travel in the car, which resulted in more anxiety.

The time after the car accident had become increasingly difficult for all of us. We were finally fortunate enough to find a play therapist, and we began attending sessions. Even after some physical healing and therapy were firmly in place, increased stress and anxiety in our home was the new normal. On one particularly challenging day at home, I pulled out a large blank journal, calling on my own experience and knowledge, and grabbed whatever was nearby. As I opened the page, my son sat next to me with his crayons, and I pointed to one side of the page as his and the other as mine.

This is how this tender-hearted work began. As we interacted together, I realized that even as an avid journal-keeper myself, I didn't feel that I could write about the effects of the accident. I believe that this feeling of not being able to put one's traumatic experience into words is present in degrees for all of us, even more so for children.

This journal became our recorder, witness, companion when we traveled, entertainer when we were out eating a meal in a restaurant, and much more. It became a soft place to land, rest, and lay out what we needed on the page without question, correction, or judgment.

That last sentence is key. Journaling with children in this context is meant to provide a place to allow the full expression of their feelings, whatever they might be, either joyful or traumatic. The journal serves as a grounding tool that provides a safe outlet to make sense of their world and enables a concrete experiential language to surface.

When my son's anxiety was high or when either of us was having a challenging time, we ended up at the kitchen table with the journal spread out between us. With little or no words, we explored and put whatever came up onto the blank page. This process is not about the perfect pens or stickers or aesthetic experience. It is about being present, giving full attention and freedom to explore the page. It is about seeing what emerges, following it, and there is no right or wrong. Not performance- or expectation-based in any way, with each journal experience unique.

Creative Journaling is not only accessible but offers a positive experiential tool that builds connection, increases communication and emotional intelligence, and helps children identify and channel their feelings and thoughts. While allowing creativity, it provides a safe place for children to trust and empowers them to discover ways to relieve and transform stress, fears, anxiety, and trauma.

Try This

6 Keys to Journaling with Children

1. **Find a large blank journal or a scrapbook that will lie flat on the table.** The journal is a container and should be kept intact. I suggest that it be large so that there is ample room to be free. Ideally, you have one page, and the child can have the other. (If no journal is possible, you can use large sheets of paper and tape them together, but a large journal is preferred to avoid ripping, losing pages, etc.)

2. **Find a special place to store this journal, somewhere reachable for the child.** Keep in mind that it is something to share only between the two of you, not something to show and tell. This is a sacred trust. For example, based on his wishes, my son was comfortable with both parents taking part. Also, it can be helpful, although not necessary, to date the page to keep track of the process.

3. **Let the child take the lead, making this journal their own.** They may want to decorate the front cover of the journal but do not push. Best not to jump to instructions or a teaching moment. Remember, this is not homework. For example, if a child draws on your side of the page, let them explore the boundary. Let the child lead, and if a conversation arises naturally, explore it. For example, when my son began to use my side of the page, I could see he was testing how I would respond, and so this began a dialogue about what is comfortable for him and me. This allowed us to discuss topics like asking permission/consent of each other, how it felt to have someone else not asking permission, etc.

4. **All mediums are welcome on the page:** pencil, felt, tape, paint, glue, multimedia, collage—anything goes. Let the child own the page, incorporating any of their "stuff" onto the page. Find ways to enhance the journal with sparkles or mud or other treasures. It is also okay to

let them explore destroying a page; it is just a page of a journal, after all. Reminder: there are no journal police.

5. **The journal is always there when you need it.** If you, the parent or caregiver, are upset or struggling with something and need a break from your day-to-day routine, take out the journal. You are the model for this process. The child learns from your approach. Remember that the process is valuable even if used only for a few minutes. This is not meant to be time-consuming. Do not force participation. The child may or may not want to join in some days.

Expectations must be put aside. No punitive measures or pressured outcomes should interfere or be connected to this activity. Try your best not to comment on what is good or what appeals to you. Instead, become curious and ask questions: What colors did you use? Do you like that color? What is that? Tell me more about that. Be present. Sometimes your nonverbal presence can be more impactful than vocal praise because it does not stop the process. Remember doing and being together is more important than the words or what is on the page.

6. **Let the child determine when the journal work finishes.** The process will usually come to a natural conclusion, or perhaps, the child will ask for a journal of their own. Remember, this is not a forced activity based on instructions and compliance.

I hope you find this useful and that journaling with your child becomes an important part of how you and your child interact, heal, and grow together.

About the Author

Nicolle Nattrass is a Certified Addiction Counselor (CAC II), playwright (PGC), professional actress (CAEA), and workshop facilitator. After twenty years as a professional actor, followed by years of frontline work as an addiction counselor, she developed four courses in Creative Journaling for Self-Care that uses a therapeutic and creative approach for clients, journal-keepers, and helping professionals. Her first book, *Just the Two of Us: A Soft Place for Tender Hearts to Land*, has been published by The Zebra Ink (Sept. 2020). She is a proud contributing author to the book *Transformational Journaling for Coaches & Clients: The Complete Guide to the Benefits of Personal Writing*, co-edited by Lynda Monk and Eric Maisel. For links to her courses and to purchase her book, visit www.nicollenattrass.com and www.iajw.org.

CHAPTER 30

Journals as Intergenerational Storytelling

By Shehna Javeed

"I would rather have a short life with width rather than a narrow one with length."

—Ibn Sina (Avicenna)

In the ephemeral fluidity of time, journals can preserve personal stories of triumphs and vulnerabilities, dark moments, and secret thoughts that we dare not share openly with others. Journals can become intergenerational transmitters of stories preserved like adored talismans across time. We can gently lean into them when we are lost or feel the urge to know ourselves more deeply. I know this now, having found my father's journal after he passed away.

At fifteen years old, in 1953 India, my father Razaul Jabbar wrote, "If you are a human being, do not touch this book without my permission. Honesty is the best policy." This quote is on the first page of a small-sized notebook (9cm x 6cm) with a jade green hardcover that includes the printed words "The Life and the Happyness" in black font, with the misspelling included and a black rose.

The diary was written by a fifteen-year-old teenage boy in 1953 over the span of three months while undergoing several operations and rehabilitation therapy in a residential hospital to correct distortions of his limbs and his body due to childhood polio. He shared his innermost thoughts and feelings as he grappled with his disability in an able-bodied world. The script is in Urdu, a dialect used in the Indian subcontinent, with Persian, Turkish, and Hindi influences and Arabic alphabets.

I am a settler, a South Asian Muslim woman who immigrated to Toronto as a child in the early 1980s. My father's lack of mobility always influenced our lifestyle. It meant embarrassingly large cars (for hand-brake space and a wheelchair), plotting a route that included ramps (or learning at an early age how to navigate a wheelchair up and down sidewalks without ramps), managing stairs, or laying and picking up towels from the floor in prep for his bath. "Normal" was different for us. While everyone admired him for his tenacity and ambition despite his disability, my emotions see-sawed between respect and frustration as he was always the center of attention.

Journals as Intergenerational Storytelling, Plaited in Language

While becoming an expert accountant, my father acquired fame as a fiction writer in Urdu, winning accolades for his work. Later in life, I realized that demonstrating expertise at numbers and words was truly impressive.

I cannot read Urdu. I cannot read his books. While I can speak Urdu fluently and without an accent, I have grade 1 reading skills. Regretfully, some things get lost in the settlement experience, and sometimes language is one of them.

I also could not read his journal, but if someone read it to me, I would fully understand it. I asked my mother to read it out loud to me. She read from the small, brown-hued pages, seated in her worn-out black armchair wearing her reading glasses. She read with ease despite the tiny writing, and after listening to a couple of entries, I realized that we needed to capture this for posterity. I started transliterating this Urdu journal using the English alphabet, turning Urdu into English.

Seeing Our Shared Humanity

It is difficult to see family members as multi-dimensional human beings, distinct from our connected roles. Like the self-centering compass in a geometry set that creates a perfect circle around the center, we judge our family members within the circle that this compass creates, where we are the center.

At times, it felt like we were reading about a stranger, and at other moments, the pages illuminated the adult that we knew. The journal entries framed the period September 10, 1953, to November 30, 1953. They often began with routine activities such as freshening up for breakfast and included nurses' names, respectfully addressed as "sisters." Other routines included "ward-washing," or the cleaning of the hospital, and visits from social workers. Several teenagers were waiting for similar operations. I was impressed with the hospital's rehabilitative therapy program to develop gross and fine motor skills through activities such as rope exercises and weights; it also included knitting, as well as academic learning and drama.

Entry date: September 16, 1953

I worked the (exercise) machine in the department. Tried to cut some wood but I was unsuccessful. I went to the massage room next. I was late ... Today six sandbags were placed on me. In the afternoon, I knitted a bit of the sweater, and looked on at the activities around the operation theater. At two p.m. came rolling class, and at four p.m. I was made to stand up. At that time, I felt sad looking at my body. Miss Kellogg visited. Patil (another resident) had his operation.

Entry date: September 25, 1953

After morning passed, I went to the department at eight a.m. Did some crochet ... Asked the driver to bring me coffee from outside. He got in trouble for bringing outside food ... The doctor said that outside food must only be brought with permission ... Evening was spent on the bed, writing a short story.

Journals Can Reveal Trauma and Extraordinary Courage

Near the end of the journal, Raza indicates homesickness after concluding two months of his nine-month stay at this hospital.

October 7, 1953

In the evening, doctor talked about the operation and said that it will be on October 21 ... After hearing this news, I felt strangely unwell. I could not sleep. In the morning, I wrote a letter to father ... I talked to Chatterjee about the chloroform. I was anxious about this all day. All evening on the bed. It was night. I am not afraid of the operation, as much as the smell of chloroform, and the discomfort that occurs before losing consciousness.

It was nine months in a hospital away from home, in another city that was an eighteen-hour train ride away, with no family around, within a culture that values closeness of family as protection and comfort, and a society that uses a deficit approach to disability. Forgotten by loved ones? Lonely? Traumatic? I knew about the operations, had heard bits and pieces of the stories, and witnessed the physical and emotional struggle at times, but the journal illuminated much more than I had known before.

After the October 21 operation, there was another operation scheduled for November 18, 1953.

November 29, 1953

Morning was difficult. Loneliness took over, and feeling very anxious since morning ... No visitors for anyone this evening.

Journals Can Be Reflective and Prescient

Journaling galvanized Raza's creativity. While still at the hospital, his first short story, "Taj Mahal," was promised for publication, and it was broadcast on the radio with a promise of ten Indian rupees in compensation. He mentioned receiving the letter from the radio station in the journal.

As we read, I began to see adult Raza's motivation for advocacy and his vigilance for equity. Systemic discrimination, both in India and Canada, barred him from career pathways; however, he learned to fight and seek justice. He fought, whether it was seeking a ramp in the condominium where we lived, or gently arguing that his wheelchair was just as clean as another man's foot when he was confronted in a place of worship on the purity of its wheels (the one who asked later apologized), or advocating for an accessible photocopier room in the workplace, free from drying umbrellas on a rainy day, or taking a case to court for human rights. I can now see how the pain of trauma was channeled toward seeking justice.

I understand that the world pitied young Raza at his physical deficit, and he wanted to resist and rise above it. Lying in his hospital bed for months, he may have wondered about his life. I believe that Raza gained independence and a strong identity because of this hospital experience, while other young men with privilege may have gained their identities by attending high-quality boarding schools.

Journaling and writing are a part of me, and I now credit my father for those passions. I write to express myself professionally or to feel the catharsis from an emotional experience. I have always been drawn to it, even though I do not identify as a writer. Releasing a written piece into the world makes me vulnerable, but I also desire it to become a thing of influence and change, almost an independent entity with its own power. I know he felt the same way.

Try This

Intergenerational Journaling: Some Tips

The Everyday

When writing, start with the routine of your day and see how it propels the ordinary into the extraordinary. Raza often started by describing the routine of the hospital, then the writing evolved into moments of insight and emotions. When I have nothing to say in my writing, I begin with the ordinary and my heart opens up to more. Writing is a living process that evolves as we begin to unravel what matters to us.

Tell a Simple Story

Was it the smile of the coffee server or the glare of the angry bus driver? Write about it. Raza wrote about another teenager who wanted to send a letter but could not find an envelope and seemed disturbed about it. Raza gave him an envelope. Between the lines, we feel the value of the envelope during a time of letter-writing, as well as Raza's generosity. Raza wrote about his simple desire for coffee from the street corner coffee shop. We can all relate to those basic yearnings, and the reader can latch on and relate to the writer.

Times, Dates, and Names Are Important

All of Raza's entries are dated, and this is meaningful to me. Raza mentioned holidays such as Gandhi's birthday, or the Hindu festival of Dasera, which brings visually appealing floating displays in road parades. My mother remembers the names of the social workers who kept in touch with him later. He mentioned a letter from an aunt whom I also knew. These references anchor the writing decades later.

Write from a Place of Authenticity

Speaking our truth in writing is ultimately the characteristic that makes journaling of deep value. Expressing his fear of the chloroform and irritation at rambunctious fellow residents makes one relate to the humanity of the experience Raza wrote about because we all have things we fear and experience those who frustrate us.

I have reflected on this journal for some time now, and it has significantly changed my perspective about my father. The smart, talented, angry, passionate, frustrating, courageous, respectful, and generous man evolved into a warm and playful grandfather. I wish I could travel through time back to 1953 to reassure this teenager that life would surpass his dreams as he traveled the world and built an accomplished life.

Raza's journal ends with words in English: "It is strange how people find time to hate when life is too short for love."

About the Author

Shehna Javeed has a flourishing career in higher education and student advising. She advocates for equity and inclusion, particularly on the understanding of the BIPOC women experiences. She volunteers for and encourages civic engagement. She enjoys writing and public speaking, and she was the TEDxUTSC speaker in 2019 with a talk titled, "Do You See People for Who They Are?" Shehna lives in Toronto with her family and can be contacted at Shehna_JournalStories@hotmail.com.

CHAPTER 31

Journaling and Creative Writing

By Diane Hopkins

"Every child is an artist. The problem is
staying an artist when you grow up."

—Pablo Picasso

Creative writing calls to many of us who possess a great love of words, reading, and books. If we don't follow that calling as we move into adulthood, in our profession, or as a hobby, at some stage later in life, we may find ourselves experiencing a creativity crisis, searching for something we feel is missing.

As most of us have been primed to pursue practical careers and treat creative activities as hobbies if we have spare time, at best, or unnecessary indulgences, at worst, we might tend to ignore our artistic urges. For those who have suppressed their inner artist, creative writing can provide an important outlet for self-expression and imagination. This can be personally therapeutic while also adding meaning and purpose to one's life.

Many journal-keepers with a creative itch will at some point ponder the idea of writing a novel or memoir. Not knowing how or where to start or feeling inadequate compared to our author heroes, we may make a few first attempts and then, unhappy with our efforts, put aside our creative desires and continue with life as normal. Until the calling comes again…

Despite clocking in many hours of writing with their journal, journal-keepers will need guidance to embody the role of creative writers—to switch their focus from writing exclusively for their discovery and healing to writing stories that entertain and engage an audience.

This chapter will guide you on the journey from journal-keeper to creative writer, showing you how to use your journaling practice to develop your creative writing skills. These lessons apply equally to aspiring memoir writers and novel writers.

Develop Your Radar for an Interesting Story

Learning how to look through your readers' eyes and find the interesting story within the vast range of stories available to you is an important skill for any creative writer. For journal-keepers, using stories from your own life is a good place to begin. You can then either collect them for a memoir or use them as inspiration to create fiction.

Think about any unusual events that have happened to you. What stands out about your life? Consider the environments you've had access to that most people wouldn't know much about; for example, working in an airport, being a lawyer, volunteering with special-needs kids, and so forth. Your life experiences can provide the backdrop for interesting stories. You might also be able to recall times when friends have shown greater interest as you've told them a story. Their interest is a sign that the details of your story might make for great content in your creative writing.

A story doesn't have to be extraordinary to be interesting, though. Stories of ordinary events or experiences, well told, can be incredibly compelling. Interesting stories are often deeply emotional ones. What were the most dramatic moments or periods of your life? The saddest?

Emotional stories engage readers because we are hardwired to feel empathy for a character going through a difficult time, and sometimes we can personally relate because we've been through something similar, and that makes us feel like we're not alone in our struggles.

Be the Character in Your Own Story

As a journal-keeper, you'll be used to writing about yourself, but as a creative writer, you'll need to write as if you were a character in a story. This will allow you to get the distance and objective perspective you'll need to write about yourself honestly, which is crucial for memoir writing and helps with writing realistic, three-dimensional fictional characters that are believable to readers.

Writing about yourself honestly means understanding how what you are thinking, feeling, and doing contribute to creating the problems you've had or how your behavior has been accentuating those problems. While journaling typically leads to discovering honest insights about ourselves, we generally still write from our own perspective.

Writing about yourself as a character elevates you to the narrator's position, and the narrator can see his or her characters with a bird's-eye view. From the narrator's position, we can more accurately assess what role we play in creating the circumstances of our lives and—importantly for storytelling—how we create meaning from those circumstances based on how we interpret everything we see, feel, and experience.

Write about Your Life Themes

The themes, or recurring topics, that run through your journal entries are significant because they are the ideas you will want to explore within the stories you write. If you write a memoir, you will need to know and intimately understand the themes that have driven that period of your life.

And if you write a novel, you will need to create characters that are guided forward in their lives by themes important to them, which will be easier and more enjoyable if they are significant to you.

Common universal themes in stories can include grief, faith, family, following your dreams, belonging, friendship, prejudice, reinvention, and resilience. Themes are particularly important in creative writing as they elevate a story from one character's singular experience to a universal struggle, which is relatable to a wider audience.

Your themes are not the same as the plot, and you'll need to look underneath the plot to discover them. For example, depending on what it means to you, getting lost on a week-long hike in the mountains (your plot) might be about the theme of resilience or faith or something else entirely.

Show More, Tell Less

Good storytelling—the kind that has an emotional impact on readers— uses writing techniques that "show" what is happening with a character, rather than relying on the narrator to "tell" the story. Showing involves using dialogue, body language, and sensory details to take the reader into the scene to feel like they are "there" with the characters.

Most journaling focuses on forms of "telling": interpretations of events, judgments of people's behavior, and labeling of emotions. We may write something like, "She was mean, I felt sad, my boss was a control freak." Creative writing asks us to show her being mean, show you feeling sad, or show the boss being a control freak.

The trick is to think in scenes. Instead of reflecting on events as if they're in the past, as we do in journaling, you need to go back into those events as if they're happening now, in the present. For example, what does your face look like when you're sad, what do you think, and/or how does your posture change?

Tame Your Inner Critic

With journaling, it's possible to write without too much self-consciousness because it's just you and your journal in a private conversation for one. But when you're writing for an audience and know that your work will be out there for others to see, you might find that your inner critic starts taking up prime real estate in your head. It might say things like what you're writing is unoriginal, it's all been done before, everyone is writing about that, what's the point, and so on. These kinds of thoughts are to be expected. It's what everyone's inner critic says when they commit to a piece of creative writing.

Taming your inner critic will need to become part of your creative writing process if you're going to finish what you've set out to write. You'll need to learn how to recognize the inner critic's thoughts as self-sabotaging and develop coping strategies for what to do when they show up. You'll also need to remind yourself that these thoughts are not necessarily true, and they're just the fearful part of you that is scared now you're moving into new—and exciting—creative territory.

Try This

1. Develop Your Radar for an Interesting Story

Review your journals or reflect on your life so far and answer the following questions:

- What material from my life would make an interesting story (for example, meeting my biological dad, the three months I spent in an ashram) or a small part of a story? (For example, my larger-than-life best friend, the strange guy I dated that summer.)
- What inner battles have I faced? What emotional challenges have I gone through? (For example, a difficult divorce, living with a chronic illness, being a perfectionist.)

2. Be the Character in Your Own Story

Review a selection of your journal entries with the lens of seeing yourself as a character. Answer the following two questions, writing in third person as if you are the narrator of the story:

- What is the character (you) struggling with? What is the core conflict? (For example, not feeling happy in her marriage, trying to belong after moving to a new community, striving to get his father's approval.)
- What is the character (you) doing to sabotage themself? (For example, people-pleasing, lashing out when she's angry, pushing away the person he loves, jumping to conclusions about what other people mean.)

3. Write about Your Life Themes

Review your journals to discover the themes that you return to again and again. These will probably be things you've struggled with or think about a lot. Make a list of your most common themes. These will form the backbone of the memoir or fictional stories you write.

4. Show More, Tell Less

Take an event you've described in your journal and rewrite it into a scene where something is happening—an action or a conversation. You could show a scene centered on a conversation that ended with you feeling a certain way (e.g., angry, sad, excited) and write it without labeling your emotions. Make sure you include dialogue and sensory descriptions (sights, smells, sounds, physical sensations) so that your readers feel like they are there with you as the event is happening.

5. Tame Your Inner Critic

Answer the following questions in your journal so that you're prepared for when your inner critic shows up:

- What thoughts do I have that try to convince me to give up on my writing? Which ones are the most persuasive?
- What will I do when these thoughts come up? (For example, don't allow them to stop me from writing, replace them with more positive thoughts)

About the Author

Diane Hopkins is a nonfiction book writing coach and editor for creatives, coaches, leaders, and entrepreneurs. She guides aspiring authors in writing memoir, self-help, and business books using personal stories to connect with their readers and inspire meaningful change. Diane also works as a speech coach and editor, helping clients turn their stories and expertise into powerful messages of transformation as invited keynotes speakers at big events, including business conferences and United Nations events, TEDx, and TEDWomen. You can learn more about her work at www.wordandwing.co and contact her at diane@wordandwing.co.

CHAPTER 32

Journaling and Design Inspiration

By Meryl Cook

"As an artist, journaling is one way of showing up for yourself. It allows you to tap into what's inside. By doing this you can make art that is a reflection of who you are. Art that has real impact."

—Meryl Cook

A journal is a great place for dreaming wildly. Letting your pen move freely and writing in your journal can help to open creativity. It's a bit like limbering up. Just like having a great conversation with a friend can inspire and help you sort through ideas, writing in your journal can be like having a conversation with yourself, where you are free to try new ideas and explore different concepts.

A journal doesn't have to be just about writing. In my journal, I incorporate many simple sketches. Others use their journals to post favorite photos, swatches of color. A journal can be a great source of design ideas.

As an artist, journaling is one way of showing up for yourself. It allows you to tap into what's inside. By doing this, you can make art that reflects who you are. Art that has real impact.

Words from your journal can become part of the design of some other artistic project. Perhaps a word crops up frequently in your journal or a word you are curious about. This word could become the design. Or you can use this word to explore the sensations associated with it. Your interpretations of these sensations can lead to design ideas.

The words from your journal can also influence your design process. For example, in a piece of textile art inspired by writing about having no boundaries, I wrote about the feeling of expansion that comes with this concept. This led me to choose colors that drew the eye outward to reinforce this sensation of expansion.

Design and Creativity Through Journaling

At a time in my life where I found myself blocked and uncertain about how to move forward, writing and sketching in a journal were a huge component of how I reinvented myself. Six months earlier, I had been diagnosed with breast cancer. At that time, I decided to leave my twenty-year practice as a homeopath. I promised myself I would allow the time and space I needed to fully heal before embarking on a new path.

The week I finished treatment in 2016, I attended a journaling and yoga workshop with author Sheree Fitch and yogi Josette Coulter. That started my journaling practice. I've been writing and sketching most days since then.

I had been a contemporary rug-hooking artist for eight years up to this point and had been designing my own rugs for seven of those years. Beginning to write and sketch in a journal transformed my design process, as well as my life. My experience was that the more I wrote and sketched, the more rug ideas flowed out of me. It was as if the act of writing released my creativity. I developed a process for journaling that got me unblocked and ready to focus on moving forward in my life and business.

In addition to helping me to shift my perspective, my journaling became directly linked to my designs. Each new design began with my journal. I wrote about what I was experiencing and what I needed from this experience. I would write about and sketch the sensation of the event I needed to create. These sketches would become my next design.

I then started to take the words from my journal that had inspired the design and write them on the linen around the outside edges of the design. These phrases became a sort of meditation as I was hooking the rug.

Each rug represented the next step that I needed to take in my healing journey. After eight months, my first seven healing mats and many of the notes from my journals became my first book *One Loop at a Time, a story of rughooking, healing and creativity*. This book was quickly followed by *One Loop at a Time, The Creativity Workbook*.

I chose the term one loop at a time for both of my books since, as a journal writer, I write longhand, the words forming one loop at a time. In rughooking, the wool strips or yarn are pulled up through the backing one loop at a time. This phrase has also come to represent to me the freedom to not have everything worked out in advance, the freedom to make changes along the way, and the freedom to get started without always knowing the result. My designs begin as simple sketches that I transfer onto the linen backing. I choose a color palette but don't color plan every area of the rug in advance. I then approach the design one loop at a time and feel free to change or reinterpret the design as I go along.

My designs continue to be inspired by my journal writing. In addition to my healing mats, I now have a series of Wild Women rugs and a Heart Notes series. My process has evolved over time. It started as a way to heal myself, with rugs such as Love Letter, Curvy Lines, Joy Releasing, Dancing Wildly, Surrender, and more.

More recent designs have been focused on how to help the world. For example, as the COVID-19 pandemic was developing around the world, I felt overwhelmed and powerless with the amount of suffering.

This quote inspired me:

> "Do not be dismayed by the brokenness of the world. All things break. And all things can be mended. Not with time, as they say, but with intention. So, go. Love intentionally, extravagantly, unconditionally. The broken world waits in darkness for the light that is you."

—L.R. Knost

I wrote about what qualities each type of love would embody and how it would look or feel to live these kinds of love. I designed and hooked a tryptic Love in the Time of a Pandemic as my response—with intention—to the world's suffering. Hooked mainly in the colors of the Heart Chakra (pink and green), I spent March and April 2020 hooking and sending love out to the world in the form of these three pieces: Unconditional, Intentional, and Extravagant.

Try This

Leaning into Joy Exercise

This is an exercise that I find inspiring and that opens up my creativity.

Write about something that brings you joy. Where do you feel it in your body? Can you draw the feeling of joy?

When you do your sketch, try not to draw just an image that reminds you of joy. Rather, try to capture the embodied sensation of what joy feels and looks like.

The next time you are out for a walk, see if you can notice five moments of joy. Don't forget to notice where you feel this joy in your body.

This practice of looking for moments of joy is important because:

* It trains your brain and body to look for joy and to recognize the feeling within you.

- It helps you to ground and be in the present moment.
- When you are looking for joy, you see it more often. This can help crowd out the negative feelings.
- By noticing the world around you more fully, you will feel inspired.

What if Exercise: Dreaming Wildly

The purpose of this "what if exercise" is to dream wildly and to tap into the body feeling. This exercise is my most popular writing prompt and the one I get the most positive feedback about!

What If? Try writing and sketching one of your wildest dreams in the form of a *what if,* as in *what if* something marvelous were to happen?

Connect to the body feeling. What would it feel like if this dream came true?

Tip: Connecting with the body feeling of a positive experience is one way to start getting unblocked. The more we practice, the easier it gets.

Suggestion: Try writing three to five *what-ifs* a day for several months. You will be amazed at what starts to happen in your life!

About the Author

Color, texture, joy, and self-compassion are the key features of Meryl Cook's beautifully crafted hooked rugs, as well as her books about her journey from homeopath to artist and journal writer. Meryl is a Journal Council member of the International Association for Journal Writing (IAJW). She is the author of two books, *One Loop at a Time: A Story of Rughooking, Healing and Creativity* (2016) and *One Loop at a Time, The Creativity Workbook* (2017). What began as a way of holding space for herself following breast cancer treatment has led Meryl to a career as an artist and writer. She also works with corporate teams to help with well-being and engagement. Meryl Cook Engagement by Design is a certified woman-owned business through WEConnect International. www.merylcook.ca.

CHAPTER 33

Journaling to Connect with Nature's Wisdom

By Jackee Holder

"But when I was on the land, I felt completely at home.
Not only did I know the birds and the trees, but they knew me."

—Robin Wallkimmerer, The Earth Mother

It was the summer of 1999, and I found myself at a crossroads in my life. I was emotionally depleted, exhausted, and spiritually bankrupt. Feeling like I had nowhere else to turn to, I got still and listened to my body urging me to get up and run.

The Wisdom of Trees

Hitting the last leg of my inaugural park run, I headed in the direction of a large, towering tree perched on the top of a small hill. The next day, I did the same thing; and by the end of my run, I found myself once again under the canopy of the same tree. Soon this became my morning practice and daily pilgrimage. It was weeks before I realized that this particular tree was one of a handful of older oak trees populating the park. In folklore, the oaks are well-known as a symbol of strength and survival, the very qualities I needed to breathe in.

Sanctuary, as I called her, turned out to be a very good listener. I noticed how open and relaxed I felt as, under her watchful gaze, I performed body prayers taught to me in seminary training. In the same way that we can have mentors in people, we can have mentors in trees. I would use this time in the tree's company to write journal entries and pose questions out loud. I would lean in to the quiet and listen, eager to hear what answers would emerge. In this space, I grew stronger and more confident in listening to and trusting my inner mentor.

Knotty problems that got me into a tangle when I sat ruminating on my sofa, unraveled when the soft fascination scientists tell us we experience in nature was at work. The forces of nature, the wind, the earth, the soil, the leaves—all of it is a perfect environment for spontaneous and often unsolicited creative thinking and problem-solving.

Metaphors in nature hang, waiting like ripe fruit or flowering blossoms, ready to be plucked, digested, or inhaled. Nature leaves clues everywhere. For example, one morning, walking past a drained riverbed, the riverbed alerted me to my early signs of an escalating feeling of exhaustion. Another day, being stopped in my tracks when a chirpy robin burst into song was an instantaneous nudge to harvest my joy in an impromptu joy list in my journal. Nature-infused questions provided luminous content for curating illuminating journal prompts. Metaphors in nature provide light on a path, helping you navigate your way through life's highs, lows, and boundless opportunities.

That's why I began always walking with a small notebook and pencil and found that I looked forward to the moment when I would perch on top of one of the tree's raised roots and scribe away in my journal. From this small seed planted over twenty-one years ago are the roots for what would become one of the most popular questions from my deck of Inner and Outer Nature cards, "What would the ancient tree have to say about your challenge right now?"

Working with Visual Images of Trees and Nature

One creative tool I found enriching is to paste pictures of different trees onto different pages of a new journal or notebook. Placing visual images of trees in my journals acted as a creative stimulant and supported my narrative and self-exploration. A black-and-white photograph of what resembled huge Horse Chestnut trees, common here in London and pasted in my journal, triggered a full-color memory of an existential moment when I was six years old. I recalled a feeling of oneness and connection to the trees, to life as I played with my doll under the loving gaze of an avenue of tall trees in a park.

One famous study by Roger Ulrich, "View Through a Window May Influence Recovery from Surgery," showed that patients with a view of a small grove of trees from their hospital room made substantially quicker and better recovery from gallbladder surgery than those who looked out onto a view of a brick wall. Viewing or drawing images of trees or scenes in nature can be a bridge between the right brain and the left brain, a holding space for when the right words are hard to come by, or your thoughts feel jumbled and confused.

As well as collecting tree images for my journals, I like to doodle and draw. More recently, while training as a therapist, I found being the only Black woman and visible person of color on the course isolating. When I could not find the words I wanted to share, my doodles and drawings spoke for me.

The Elements of the Four Seasons

Noticing the seasons in nature is a natural way of staying connected to the seasons of emotions experienced daily. Begin by observing nature through the seasonal lens of the environment you are in. Observe a tree through the seasons. Take photographs or write about when it flowers, when its leaves fall, and its branches are bare.

This practice is a reminder of the seasonality of emotions experienced daily. Take this a step further by posing yourself a seasonal question in your journal or notebook. Consider the guiding principles of the current environmental season you are in. How and where are aspects of the current season's qualities reflected in your own life? How might bringing more of the seasonal energy into your life best support you right now?

Internal Weather Report

Another way I work with nature is to use the weather to connect with emotions and feelings. In her book *The Right to Write*, Julia Cameron opens each chapter with a daily weather description. The image of a washed-out gray sky may express the lingering despair you're feeling. Describing the color of the sky as it relates to your emotions and feelings often makes it easier to own what feels difficult.

Pausing and taking a moment to absorb a scene in nature can plug you into wonder and elation, as it did when I witnessed a vibrant orange sunset whilst driving home one evening from work across the inner-city horizon. Try this journal prompt: Describe your current feelings and emotions in the form of a weather report.

I am reminded of an avenue of pine trees overlooking the lake close to my home, who, on closer inspection, are descendants of some of the oldest trees in the world. The pine tree's resilience and ability to survive and thrive in poor soil conditions is not lost on me. This provoked a question about my resilience, which you may wish to give a try.

Write about a time, place, or circumstance in your life or work where you not only survived but thrived. What contributed to your resourcefulness and resilience at the time? The powerful imagery of the steadfast pine trees allowed me to connect with my resilience and strengths that often went unnoticed. Naming it and writing it down helped me to see what was there and to own it.

Try This

When You Want to Remember

Describe a tree from your past or your present that has meaning or significance for you. What is it about this tree that appeals to you? What would you say are the strong qualities of your chosen tree? Where in yourself do you locate any of these strong qualities? How could you bring more of these qualities into your working or personal life?

When You Want a Different Perspective

Select a tree image from a Google search, book, painting, or photo. Describe the tree as if you were the tree. What season is your tree in? What parts of your tree are visible, and what parts are invisible as it relates to you? How far down do your tree roots go? How much farther would you like them to go? What is the condition of the soil around your tree? What nutrients is your tree in need of? What would be different if you were deeply rooted in your life? What would be possible from this place?

When You Want to Go Deeper

Describe one of your favorite places in nature. Now apply these two questions exquisitely posed by the writer Robert Macfarlane to unearth further insights, drawing from the wisdom of your chosen landscape: "What do I know when I'm in this place that I can know nowhere else?" and "What does this place know of me that I cannot know of myself?"

When You Want to Respond to the Climate Change Crisis

In her novel *The Twelve Tribes of Hattie*, Ayana Mathi shares a memorable line, "She smelled the absence of trees before she saw it." Use this prompt to write a love letter to the trees where you state your case for why we must protect the trees. Remind yourself of all that trees do for us and the environment. Paint a picture of a world without trees and the impact on us and the environment.

About the Author

Jackee Holder celebrates the beauty of trees and nature in inner cities and towns through the practice of writing, journaling, facilitation, and speaking. She is the co-author of the pocket-sized, illustrated *Writing with Fabulous Trees Writing Map*, *The Inner & Outer Nature Self-Discovery Card Deck*, *49 Ways to Write Yourself Well*, and *Be Your Best Life Coach*. Jackee is an award-winning coach and coach supervisor who works out of the UK. Connect with Jackee over at www.jackeeholder.com, at Instagram @ jackeeholderinspires, or by email info@jackeeholder.com.

CHAPTER 34

Journaling and Traveling

By April Bosshard

*"We write to taste life twice:
in the moment and in retrospection."*

—Anais Nin

At twenty-three, I took my first solo road trip down the coast of California, following the Pacific Coast Highway. I took my time, staying in B-and-Bs and cheap hotels. My journal pages captured the questions of my life at the time: What is my purpose? What does it mean to live an authentic, creative life?

Less than a year later, at twenty-four, with similar questions in mind, I packed everything into storage and headed off to travel in Southeast Asia for a minimum of six months. I had an open ticket and, honestly, no idea when I would return. I was leaving my family and a good relationship, but I felt pulled to wander the world for a while. I wrote this in my journal on my departure day:

> As I walked to the gate, choking back tears, I reminded myself that for the next many months the writer within would be my connection to home, a tool, a power, and that was a comfort.

My journal was a comfort on that trip, especially when, weeks after departing, I discovered I was pregnant. My journal pages captured my surprise and sorrow until I was ready to accept and embrace the next stage of my life.

A journal is an ideal traveling companion—one who always listens and rarely talks back. I never leave home without one. The more trips I take and the farther afield I go, the more important the practice of journaling becomes to me.

A journal is especially valuable when traveling alone, but it can also be a personal refuge when traveling with others. Journaling as a practice can also be shared with one's traveling companions.

In 2008, I traveled to France with my husband and two daughters, then ten and twelve. For the trip, they each chose a journal to record experiences. One balmy night, we toted our journals to the top of the Eiffel Tower. We found a tight corner out from underfoot of the crowds and wrote together as the city of lights sparkled below. We received a few strange looks, but we captured those magical moments in the sky, and we each have our words to look back on.

Memories are fallible. Journaling retains experiential details that allow past experiences to have renewed life in the present, reflective moment. Photos provide accurate records of people and places, but without some form of journaling, even on the backs of the photos, the details of the event, especially thoughts and feelings, are lost over time.

A journal is a relationship with time. Each entry marks its own time and date stamp, and over years, over decades, these individual days reveal patterns of thoughts and feelings that provide a rich resource for understanding oneself.

No matter how objective your notes might be, a journal captures *your* perceptions of experiences. You write down what *you* notice, perceive, and react to, so the contents of your journal are always subjective. Through journaling, you stay closer to the facts of what happened than memory. At the moment, we believe we can count on memory, and maybe a snapshot or two, but as moments pile up, memories fade and jumble, losing their clarity until they become a dreamy general backdrop to a once detail-rich adventure.

On my way to Southeast Asia, I spent a week on the big island of Hawaii. I wrote this on one of my days there:

Feb 2nd, 1995, Waipio Valley, HA:

Sitting on the beach I was eating a papaya. There was a man sitting not far away and he yelled out, "Hey!" I looked around and there was a wild horse directly behind me about five feet away. He was definitely sneaking up on me! I offered him the remains of my papaya, which he slurped up immediately. He hovered a bit longer to see if I had anything else before wandering off.

As I read these words now, that day emerges from the past and impacts my present. I taste that papaya twice.

In the spring of 2017, my wanderlust surfaced again, and I took another long trip by myself. I called it a creative sabbatical, or a midlife gap year. This time I left behind two nearly grown daughters and husband, from whom I was temporarily separated, who understood my need to travel but didn't particularly like being left behind.

June 17th, 2017, Brittany, France:

On the pink granite coast above Trégieur. C— brought me here. A gorgeous, peaceful, magical place. A beautiful day—sunshine, mild, blue skies. The rocks are pinkish, yellowish, the sea looks turquoise. The sound of its lapping a balm for the soul. Had a short snooze in the grass that edges up to the rocks. Clumps of pink thrift everywhere and tiny low growing broom, or maybe it's a type of clover with a yellow flower. The landscape here, on a day like today, is idyllic. I fell asleep thinking (at C—'s prompting): "What do I need to bring in to my life in the next 6 months?"

Traveling solo at forty-seven wasn't quite the same as at twenty-four. My journal was a welcome and necessary companion.

June 23rd, 2017, Brittany, France:

I'm aware of my aloneness more and more, not just because of arising inner moods, but also in the looks I get from some people. Very few people travel alone it seems to me. At a place like this there are mostly couples, some elderly, or couples traveling as friends, or as families.

People look at me sitting or eating alone and I think they are wondering. There is a veiled curiosity. I am an anomaly and I stand out, but the gazes are for the most part surreptitious. For some of the women, their second, third, or fourth gaze betrays some longing. One glanced at her husband after, as if assessing.

Beyond the surprise and the curiosity there emerges a tentative generosity. Perhaps a restrained French version, silent and subtle, of "You go, girl."

All this to say that what I'm doing isn't "normal" and there is a temptation to think it's not right. But the stubborn rebel in me replaces "normal" with "usual" and conjures up the French saying, "Vive la différence!"

After six months in Europe, a brief return trip to Canada, and a conference presentation in Mexico, I circled back to France to attend an artists' residency in the spring of 2018.

By this time, I'd filled many journals with my adventures, but during the month-long residency, my days were focused more on painting than on writing. So, for my journaling practice, I captured "moments" at the end of each day. No matter how tired I was, I wrote down at least six things, and I told myself they only had to make sense to me.

April 27th, 2018, Orquevaux, France:

*—the beautiful huge bunch of lilacs Marie's mother brought today
(all the lilacs in bloom right now)*

*—taking the paddleboat out with Vikki this afternoon and
getting stuck in the boathouse! (the goats and the run-down
caretaker's house)*

*—another yummy Marie dinner and everyone sitting at the table by
candlelight while a nearly full moon was on the rise above the
hills outside*

—working on a self-portrait today. Challenging but a good practice.

*—nice talk with Leo and Josh (talking to Leo about life and death
and keeping negative thoughts at bay). Leo shirtless at the sink
this morning*

—chocolate pie and ice cream at midnight

The questions I had carried in my heart along California's coast at the age
of twenty-three were still with me as I wandered the halls of a château
in rural France decades later. But I'd lived some of my answers by then. I
knew this because of journaling, especially journaling while traveling.

Traveling expands our awareness of the world. Journaling while
traveling expands and deepens our awareness of ourselves and of life
in general. We touch into a deep wisdom within when we journal. This
sometimes leads to transcendent insights that cut through specific times
and places and remind us of the wonder of being alive.

At the end of the painting residency, I wrote myself this message, still
potent as I read it today:

April 28th, 2018, Orquevaux, France:

*No day is to be squandered. Each one is a gift of fleeting possibilities.
Seize one, unravel it, make something in it and of it. Be the creator*

you were born being. Each day you think is nothing or something will surprise you with its mystery (if you let it). Every urge is life moving through you. Be consumed by each day. Fall into bed ravished.

Try This

When journaling while traveling, I suggest the following:

- Focus on your senses. They are the "facts" that make moments come alive again later.
- Write some parts as scenes—describe action and dialogue as if they're happening in front of you.
- Describe people, even if you don't know them.
- Record snippets of dialogue—yes, eavesdrop!
- Record details such as restaurant and street names, even metro stops.
- Collect bits of physical evidence that could be added to the journal, such as museum and train ticket stubs.
- Carry extra pens. They always seem to run out of ink at the most inopportune times.
- Write down dates and locations at the top of each entry. Maybe even the time of day.
- Include little sketches here and there, even if you don't think of yourself as an artist.
- Always be honest in your journal. Your Future Self will appreciate this.
- Choose a size, shape, and weight of journal that you are comfortable carrying in a bag or tote bag. You want it with you almost all the time. Try to open it every day while on the road. If you don't have much time, write down six "moments" that capture a detailed essence of some of your experiences.

About the Author

April Bosshard is a writer, story coach, and creator of Deep Story Design. She helps writers all over the world navigate the personal and creative challenges that arise while working on long-form narrative projects, such as novels, screenplays, and memoirs. Find out more: www.deepstorydesign.com.

CHAPTER 35

Journaling to Find Love

By Kim Ades

"The greatest love story is the one that begins and ends in your mind. Start by writing it down and give it a beautiful unfolding."

—Kim Ades

At thirty-nine years old, I had already been married for fifteen years and divorced for four. If you did the math correctly, I got married at the age of twenty. After having two kids and doing everything I could to make it work, it all went up in flames. We were a young and hopeful couple who put a lot of effort into a relationship that ultimately was not meant to be.

Divorce left me as a single mother without a lot of dating experience. I ventured into the dating scene with my training wheels on, rocking side to side without much balance, experimenting with this thing called "online dating." I met a heap of different men, and I went on a slew of first, second, and even third dates. None of those men turned out to be my type.

I had a friend named Mike who, after having a near-death experience, acquired this other-worldly ability to connect with spirits and gather information that was inaccessible to the rest of us. He could look into someone's eyes and receive a download of personal information. He would know if they were sick, hiding something, and what their nature was like. Every time I met a new man, I would send Mike a picture before my date, and he would provide me with feedback on the feasibility of each match.

He would come back each time with comments like: "You're kidding, right?" or "Definitely not."

Eventually, I did meet someone. I became involved in a long-distance relationship with a man that I was convinced was a perfect match for me. After about six months, I sent Mike a picture just to make sure. His reply? "There's an 80 percent chance that this man is not for you." Stunned with his assessment, I told him that he must have made a mistake and just needed to talk to the fellow, and he would change his mind. Mike agreed, spoke to him, and came back with the following report: "There's an 85 percent chance that this man is not for you."

Initially I resisted Mike's findings, but a couple of months later, the relationship came to its natural conclusion. Still, I was determined to find the right man. I knew he had to be out there somewhere. As an avid journaler, I decided to journal about my ideal man—his physical features, personality, and behavior—in as much detail as possible. I took this seriously. I journaled regularly and wrote about his warmth, his social graces, and his gift with kids. I described his ability to get along with my family, his willingness to live a life filled with adventure, and his undying love for me. The picture in my mind was unfolding.

And then one day this happened...

We celebrated my son's twelfth birthday party at a downtown improv spot with a small group of his closest friends. At the end of the evening, I packed all the kids I was responsible for into my van and forgot the one boy whose parents were supposed to pick him up. I left him there, outside the improv theater, alone.

I couldn't shake my guilt. I was churning and burning and beating myself up. How could I be so negligent? What kind of mother does that? What I did was unforgivable. Even though I spoke to the mother and made sure that her son was safe with an adult and pleaded for forgiveness, the nightmare just wouldn't leave me; and that night, I couldn't sleep. The vision of this poor boy standing in the streets, alone and terrified, haunted me. I felt awful, and I knew, that without relief, I would have many more sleepless nights.

As an executive coach who deals with many guilt-related issues with clients, I decided to try a little self-coaching. What would I tell my clients to do in the same situation? I would tell them to "trade up." Think of a slightly better thought and then think of one that's better than that. Think about something that makes you feel good; change the subject if you need to.

I decided to apply my own advice, and to turn my attention to something else, I decided to journal about my ideal partner again. I began with a conversation with God.

"Okay, God, I am ready for you to bring me the man of my dreams. I am here waiting. Tell him to just come and get me because I'm ready. Make him warm, and kind, and loving, and make him great with kids. Also, God, make sure that we have similar values and that my family likes him. Please make him the kind of guy who knows, without a shadow of a doubt, that I am what he wants and make him very comfortable expressing that regularly. I hope I am not being too demanding, God, but please make sure he is attractive and not too short."

I continued my fantasy by writing an imagined conversation in my journal. It was brief, but it felt incredibly real:

"Hello?" (answering the phone)

"Hi, Kim? My name is Jake (I always liked that name). I got your number from my colleagues at work, and they said that I had to call you because they said that you were my perfect match. They said that if I didn't call you that I would be missing the opportunity of a lifetime to meet my soulmate."

For whatever reason, that imaginary conversation left me with such a strong feeling, that I shared it with a friend of mine a few days later. That same evening, I arrived home to find a message waiting for me on my voicemail:

"Hi, Kim? My name is Allan. I got your name from a couple of teachers at the school where I teach. They are under the impression that we should meet."

Holy smokes! My fantasy had come to life! My heart was doing triple somersaults! I called him right back, and without any censoring, I told him my story—about the boy I left alone downtown, the guilt, and my fantasy journal. I was risking the possibility that he might think I was insane, but I couldn't help myself. I was completely overwhelmed with the turn of events.

He asked me to join him for dinner on Saturday night. Unfortunately, I had a scheduled speaking engagement in Ohio on Saturday morning and my flight home was only landing at 5:30 p.m. Calculating the time that it would take to arrive, cross customs, pick up my luggage, get home and freshen up, I suggested a later dinner at 8:00 p.m. He asked me how I was planning on getting home. I said that I would grab a cab. He said, "How about if I pick you up?"

An airport pickup on the first date?!

"Sure!" I said, "I would love that. How will I know it's you?"

"I have some pictures on Facebook that you can take a look at."

Finding pictures of him surrounded by what looked like his students, I thought he was pretty attractive. To be sure that my enthusiasm wasn't premature, I immediately sent the pictures to Mike and waited for his reply.

"This one looks good," he said. "He has a good heart, and he's got rhythm."

I got a green light from Mike!

On the flight home from Ohio, I wrote in my journal:

"I am meeting Allan today, and for some reason, I am not nervous. It feels normal. After seeing his pictures, I feel like I have met him before. I am not sure where; maybe in another life. And for the first time in forever, there will be someone waiting at the airport when I land."

I landed. I collected my luggage. I took a deep breath. And as I walked through the solid glass doors into the arrival area, there he was, waiting for me, with a handmade sign with a big smiley face and my name on it.

He felt familiar, as though I had known him forever. He was definitely attractive and a little short (you always get what you focus on).

Within a week, he told me he loved me and started dropping hints about marriage. Six months later, we were engaged and planning a wedding. That was nearly fourteen years ago.

Journaling helped me define what I was looking for so that when it showed up, I could easily identify it. Journaling also helped me lift my spirits when things were not going as planned. Journaling was the tool that allowed me to turn my attention to what I wanted instead of focusing on what was happening, and it prepared me for meeting my soulmate.

Try this

Here are some tips for journaling to help you find love:

1. Describe your ideal partner in as much detail as you can—their appearance, personality, attitudes, and behaviors.
2. Write down an ideal conversation between you and your potential partner. When it feels real and leaves you feeling enthusiastic, you know you've written something ideal and are ready for it to show up in your life.
3. While waiting for the ideal partner to step into your life, pay attention to other couples. Notice what you love about them and journal your observations.

I hope that your journaling experience leads you to all the love you want and deserve!

About the Author

Kim Ades (pronounced Add-iss) is the president and founder of Frame of Mind Coaching™ and The Journal That Talks Back™. Recognized as an expert in thought mastery and mental toughness, Kim uses her unique philosophy and coaching style to help business owners and leaders identify their blind spots and shift their thinking to yield extraordinary results. Author, speaker, entrepreneur, coach, and mom of five, Kim teaches her powerful Frame of Mind Coaching™ methodology to leaders, executives, coaches, and parents worldwide using journaling as the foundation of her process. Kim has been featured in a variety of online publications, including Forbes and Inc., and has spoken for organizations including Microsoft Canada, TEC Canada, Vistage, EO, HRPA, and SHRM. In addition to being interviewed on many top-ranking podcasts, Kim hosts a podcast called *The Frame of Mind Coaching™* and invites leaders from all over the world to be coached live on the show.

www.frameofmindcoaching.com

www.thejournalthattalksback.com

CHAPTER 36

Journaling and the Lost Words

By Marisé Barreiro

"The entire path of our personal journey is shaped by a tug-of-war between our desire to forget and our desire to remember."

—Philip Shepherd

There are so many ways in which we live in circles. We circle the sun and circle around our story. Not unlike the concentric records that trees keep hidden inside, each year that we live creates an outer frame for our previous story, highlighting certain threads in the tapestry of our life that were not obvious before.

The distinctive color and shape of the current chapter reveal new patterns by similarity and contrast and by adding space around our formative experiences: those that keep haunting us and whispering in our ears year after year, circle after circle.

Being fully in the present goes hand in hand with seeing the past with fresh eyes.

I have lived most of my life in the seaside town where I was born, at the Galician Lower Bays. At the beginning of October, I met my local writing group at the start of the path to the hills that shelter our town from the north wind. That hill range happens to be the territory of my childhood. We walk in silence and write about what we see and feel.

There are hollow boulders with rain puddles inside, furze and heather, moss and broom. The sight is breathtaking, over the town rooftops and into the dreamy, hazy sea, with the city of Vigo across the bay. We arrive at a stone on one of the summits that looks like an elephant in shape and size, giving that hill the popular name of Monte do Elefante. It has been a long time since I last visited this place, and I am struck anew by the totemic quality of this big boulder, its fierce presence, as if an alert creature was noticing us from inside.

After all, this is Celtic countryside, inhabited by presences and full of buried, spell-bound treasures and passageways that you'd better leave alone. We sit in a circle nearby, and as they write, I look around and reminisce.

I remember spending hours each day roaming these very paths with my two younger brothers or just with our dog, entering a state of expansive timelessness that only dusk or our mother's callings for dinner would dispel. I recall vividly the deep absorption, the freedom of being myself in that world of scent and touch and color. This place is magic, I conclude, and this elephant is somehow one of my mentors. Sadly, I forgot as I grew up, became trapped in the fog of adolescence, tried hard to be sensible and invisible as a young person until I was exhausted, and my real quest began.

I feel so grateful to be accompanied by this bunch of writerly souls who pour their hearts on the page with every prompt I offer. One of them, a retired nurse eleven years older than me, used to volunteer to take me out in my pushchair as a toddler when my mother was busy. Living at your birthplace makes you bump into your old self at every turn. You are given the choice to forget or to remember daily. When I finally abandoned the invisibility pretense and lifted my eyes from the ground, I was surprised to be surrounded by people who knew everything about me, not to mention about my parents and grandparents.

Shortly before I became a writing facilitator in 2009, I was lucky to attend one of the last workshops taught in Europe by Mauricio and

Rebecca Wild, the founders of Pestalozzi School in Ecuador, probably the most prestigious nondirective school of all times. I was in awe at how finely tuned they were to the developmental needs of children and teens, using careful observation and trial-and-error experimentation as they created a rich variety of materials suited for each age. They trusted and followed the children's impulses according to their own inner compass as the organizing principle of the whole curriculum.

One of the stories they shared touched me deeply and still ripples through my teaching today. That was the story of how they changed their minds about teenagers as they were researching what their true needs might be. They had no previous experience with teens, so they began by offering them the most stunning creative projects, such as restoring an old railway and locomotive and then taking a journey together to observe and adjust according to their reactions.

Some of those projects were successfully carried out, and others were not, but what the Pestalozzi teachers found remarkable is that the teens became energized and busy for short spans of time, and then sat down again just to talk and talk, absorbed in deep conversations. Over time they concluded that adolescence's most important developmental task is talking.

I held my breath: as a secondary school teacher, I had spent the last twenty years perfecting the art of keeping my students silent.

Rebecca told us seriously: adolescence is when one must find the link between one's heart and one's words. Our students, in a safe environment, would spend hours gazing into each other's eyes and finding words to match the emerging inner life, the loss of childhood, the tender sexual feelings, the thrill of the future in their hands. They were in no hurry, delving in that liminal place for a long, long time.

Rebecca added that the consequence of not finding that heart-word link is tragic: it condemns us to live a lie. Then she paused, letting her words sink in. I was flooded by memories of my teen self, shame-bound and dissociated. By then, in my forties, I had already started a writing practice and discovered a well of endless life-giving words for myself. I would start writing in a state of confusion and exhaustion and emerge clear, energized, and ready to meet life. I would deliberately seek the words that would make me physically tremble, words like lightning bolts that would dispel my lethargy and make me jump, weep, or laugh out loud.

Writing is a royal way to reestablish that lost connection between heart and word and develop a language of intimacy that flows from the heart and pours out into the conversation that we keep with the whole world. Whenever I meet a skeptical writing student, I remember that my main task is to hold the faith that they have a well inside, too—one they can tap into if they persevere.

Their apparent disinterest in their writing is forgetfulness. Every time we are silenced, every time we hand in a written work to someone who will have the final say, we give away the power of our words, our stories, until we forget. We learn to play it safe and repeat as we are told, with an enormous cost in authenticity.

Sometimes teens roll their eyes or yawn theatrically when I visit schools and nudge them to write differently. But often, they end up surprised by the power of their own words. They cannot hide their satisfaction and pride, no matter how hard they try.

I recently discovered a beautiful poem book by Robert Macfarlane and Jackie Morris called *The Lost Words,* with an unusual backstory. Each poem is an invocation aiming to bring back one of the words suppressed from the Oxford Junior Dictionary in the 2007 edition, all of them belonging to the natural world that used to be the realm of children. Words such as acorn, fern, magpie, bramble, or dandelion had been replaced by technological terms: a whole semantic field erased from one of the most popular dictionaries in the world.

A child without language for the natural world is under a dark spell, unable to name the life that sustains them. They are probably neurologically weakened as well. That is why this book is so brilliant, so well targeted with its magical outlook. It is also a powerful metaphor for journaling because every time we write and reminisce, we reclaim our own lost words, the ones that were deleted and we still ache for.

Back at Monte do Elefante, I ask the group the words they feel are missing in their lives. They write about their natural surroundings when growing up, a grandmother's old-fashioned saying or even a whole different language, since our country has quite a few that overlap geographically, often in conflicting ways. Some mention the language of innocence, simplicity, silence. Then they have a go at writing their own invocations just before dusk.

The act of writing itself works as a powerful invocation of a deeper level of personal truth. Every text we create from a mindset of discovery has certain lines that stand out for their depth and aliveness, sparking our curiosity. These are the thresholds into the realm of lost words. They appear when, as we focus on shaping signs on the page to match our experience, our breathing deepens, releasing our tensions. This allows the body to guide the process with its natural, wild intelligence, receptive to the deep undercurrents of the present moment.

If language is a collective creation that both reflects and shapes our dialogue with life, then we must have the power to make it wild again. We just need to pause, breathe, and remember.

Try This

1. Write about the tug-of-war between your desire to forget and your desire to remember. Be gentle with yourself.
2. Create a list of relationship verbs (e.g., give, embrace, forgive, welcome, share, argue, touch, let go, take, ask, leave). Let each word evoke feelings and sensations in your body. Write to uncover its potential to deepen your conversation with yourself, other people, and the natural world.

About the Author

Marisé Barreiro is a Galician writer, expressive writing facilitator, and Gestalt therapist with a degree in language and literature. You can contact her via her website: www.escribientes.es.

CHAPTER 37

Journaling for Personal Growth

By Sandra Marinella

"Our words create us. Our stories create us.
Our journal writing, I have learned, can recreate us!"

—Sandra Marinella

Personal journaling can serve as a powerful tool for personal growth and meaning. As a long-time writing teacher, I experienced many traumatic experiences while teaching high school, including the brutal shooting of a beloved student. In this chapter, I share how my personal journal writing not only allowed me to release my pain on paper and find my resilience and renewal, but also how I shared journaling as a personal growth process with my students.

Can Journaling Change Your Life? Can It Light a Path to Personal Growth?

Journals have been with us for as far back as we can trace writing. Humans have used them for release, catharsis, problem-solving, healing, personal growth, and ultimately personal transformation. Twenty years ago, Lucas, a light-hearted, energetic student who lit up my classroom with his questions, taught me that your personal journal can transform you. I share this story as a tribute to Lucas.

My Story

As a young high school teacher, I embraced journaling not only for my personal use, but I began using journaling every day in all five of my high school classrooms. I started each class with five or possibly ten minutes devoted to exploring a thought, idea, or reading. The experience helped transform my teaching into Socratic dialogue, and it helped my students become reflective, careful thinkers and participants in meaningful discussion. Our journaling and discussions helped us learn and grow each day.

In 2012, when I made the journey through my breast cancer and my son's difficult cancer, I wrote copious notes in my journal. As I recovered from a double mastectomy, I was struck by how journaling works. In my cancer journal, I scrawled, *"Our words create us. Our stories create us. Our journal writing can recreate us."*

I began digging through closets and unearthed twenty-seven journals. I am not a prolific journal writer, but the journals I had kept since age nine held powerful insights. I left full-time teaching and committed myself to researching and writing about the gifts writing can give us, especially if we learn to understand and use our journals intentionally for personal growth.

From my stack of old journals, I realized that I used journaling for documenting my existence as a child. For discovering my voice as a teen. For catharsis when I fell in or out of love. But I also learned as I grew into adulthood that I used journaling to help work my way out of an idea stuck in my head, a rumination. Once I began to recognize this pattern in myself, I began to consciously change that pattern and approach rumination as a problem to be solved. Journal writing became a great tool for this. As I have aged, I have come to see my journal writing as largely for reflection and personal growth.

How Does This Work?

While stages are rarely definitive, I realized a pattern that I often see writers use to tackle personal pain and come to accept and personally grow from their journal writing. I observed this in my classrooms and in ongoing workshops with writers, veterans, and cancer patients. Here is the pattern:

- Experiencing pain and grief
- Breaking the silence
- Accepting and making sense of our stories
- Rewriting and finding the meaning in our stories
- Personal growth

The Story of Lucas

My student Lucas will show us how this works. Lucas was always the first student who bound into my classroom for second-period Humanities. He teased me about my car, and I teased him about his green t-shirt sporting a German phrase I did not understand. His positive energy lit up the room. Indeed, Lucas was well-loved inside and outside of our classroom.

One Monday, I dashed up the steps past the metal gates at my high school to be greeted by a counselor. "Lucas was shot," she blurted. My legs buckled beneath me. I dropped my stack of books, and my essays scattered across the linoleum.

Lucas was murdered on a Sunday. On that Monday, my high school found itself unexpectedly knuckled under with the weight of shock. Two counselors came into my classroom, and as gently and calmly as possible, they told the story. Lucas worked at a nearby Walmart. That Sunday afternoon, a security guard had caught someone walking out the front door of the store with a TV. On a whim, the guard asked Lucas if he wanted to ride along as he tracked down the thief. With Hollywood chase scenes likely flickering through their minds, Lucas said, "Sure."

The two justice-seekers jumped into an aging Chevy, completely unsuited for chase scenes, and followed the robber several miles until he pulled into an empty church parking lot. The chase car also pulled in and stopped. Then the thief pulled a gun out of his glove compartment, approached their car, and shot first the guard and then Lucas in the head. Both died instantly.

Experiencing Pain and Grief

The trauma created by this story rocked my classroom for weeks. Young minds, all minds, need time to absorb and learn to live with a shock. Both time and silence help us experience our pain and grief. There were, indeed, long moments of silence after the counselors spoke, and many tears. While we usually wrote in class, we did not write that day or for several days. When a traumatic event happens, it is best to let it settle before turning to our writing.

Breaking the Silence

Ten days later, after an all-school memorial for Lucas, I wanted my students to have a chance to share their thoughts. For ten minutes, we wrote in our journals about Lucas and the gratitude we held for him. This led to a meaningful talk about losing our friend and a decision to create a journal filled with our memories of Lucas for his family. It was difficult to break our silence, but we wanted to honor Lucas, and talking about him and creating our journal helped us move forward toward healing.

Accepting and Making Sense of Our Stories

Each student contributed one page to our gift journal. We compiled poems, songs, and journal stories holding precious memories. There were three photos and a beautiful watercolor piece showing the lanky boy in the green t-shirt. It became the book's cover. The book helped us stitch this painful memory into our lives in a healthy way. After we delivered our journal to Lucas' grateful family, we created a small space by the assignment box where we left remembrances to Lucas as needed—a key chain, a photo of his car, and often, flowers. While we could not make sense of why anyone would murder our dear Lucas, we could learn to honor and live with our loss.

Rewriting and Finding the Meaning in Our Stories

A final memory of Lucas helped me find a thread of meaning that I could hold inside to bear this loss. The week before Lucas died, we had been reading Saint-Exupery's *The Little Prince*. The story centered on a pilot who landed in the Sahara Desert. Having a mechanical problem, he set about repairing his plane when the odd, childlike Little Prince appears. Initially, the Little Prince is quite put off by the pilot, who is completely wrapped up in his airplane repairs. But slowly, the Little Prince uses his magical stories to befriend the pilot and teach him important lessons about life. During one of our classroom discussions about the book, I asked, "What have you learned?"

"The fox came up from his hole!" All eyes turned toward the fourth row. Lucas. "That fox teaches us about trust and friendship. Powerful stuff. But the best part is the fox's gift. He gave the Little Prince a quote, a thought." Then Lucas paused, knowing his silence would give this quote the emphasis it needed. *"What is essential is invisible to the eye,"* he said. "This quote is cool—and I like the idea of giving free gifts, too!" he joked. Then sitting side-saddle at his desk, Lucas poised himself like Rodin's *Thinker*. He held our attention. "The invisible is the best stuff—goodness, truth, friendship, stuff like that! Incredibly important," he added. Then Lucas turned and leaned forward on this desk, leaning into a future that should have been.

Personal Growth

That was the last vivid memory I have of Lucas. I rediscovered this story in my journal several weeks after his death. I had written about it, remembered it, reread it, and reflected on the power of it in my heart. In writing, framing, and reframing, we learn to hold our stories in new and bearable ways that allow for personal growth and even transformation. While the loss of Lucas was painful, it grew me in the face of grief, and it allowed me to embrace and honor with more reverence all that is truly remarkable in our lives—love, hope, friendship. Even Lucas. I hold his memory dear.

Personal journaling can grow and change us throughout our life journey. It is the most powerful force of personal change in my life.

Try This

Personal Growth Writing Prompts

Free-write your responses, including your thoughts and feelings, to any of these questions.

1. What book has changed you the most? What did you learn from it?
2. Who do you know who has changed your life in an uplifting way? What gratitude do you hold in you for this special person?
3. What turning point in your life has changed you the most? What did you learn?
4. What challenge has taught you the most? How did this experience grow you?

Later come back to this writing. Reflect on it and explore your new insights and learning.

This chapter draws upon materials from *The Story You Need to Tell—Writing to Heal from Trauma, Illness, or Loss*. Copyright © 2017 by Sandra Marinella. Used with permission from the author and New World Library.

About the Author

Sandra Marinella is an award-winning writing teacher and author. She has taught writing and story-sharing to thousands of students, professionals, veterans, and cancer patients. When she faced cancer, she wrote *The Story You Need to Tell*, an acclaimed and inspirational guide on writing to heal and transform. She teaches at Integrative Health at Mayo Clinic in Phoenix, where a study has established the effectiveness of her methods to reduce stress and pain and to dramatically improve moods and well-being. She speaks and gives workshops on the power of our stories and personal writing to heal and grow our lives. You can learn more at www.storyyoutell.com or write her at sandra@storyyoutell.com.

CHAPTER 38

Journaling for Dream Fulfillment

By Joyce Chapman

"Life is a daring adventure, or nothing."

—Helen Keller

I welcome you to open up to the adventure of a lifetime. In this journey, you are the star, you make all the decisions, and you can go solo or share your adventure with others.

Growing older is one of life's privileges. Growing wiser and more joyful is optional. Journaling is your take-off point for one of the most exciting journeys you can ever embark upon—the journey into yourself. You will be your own personal tour guide and will experience laughter, tears, memories, and letting go.

It is the path to traveling through your past, acknowledging your present, and creating your future. You will take a close look at who you are now and what you want in your life, coaxing your deep inner knowing to come out into the open. You will assume your rightful position as the main character in your own life. The journaling process as a tool for mindfulness training will support you in determining your future out of conscious choice rather than random actions.

My journaling journey began many decades ago with a single decision. A key success factor in taking a next step with a new dream as a school administrator was creating effective written communications. Rather than register for a traditional business writing course, I fed my creativity by attending a journal workshop. *Why not?* I thought. I was never known for being traditional but rather a dreamer who always had new dreams to pursue and realize.

Honestly, I was drawn to the workshop, hoping to be freed from my fear of writing for others. I didn't have a clue about the Pandora's Box that was about to pop open for me! I had always spent time philosophizing and creating in various ways, but I had never applied those skills to thinking about myself and recreating my life. I left the first day of the class consumed by the revelation that I had never paid close attention to my life.

The truth hit me with a huge impact. I started to think about myself in depth and realized that if I couldn't understand myself, I couldn't love myself. I didn't know exactly who was there to love. I was taking care of the business of life, and there was no time for studying myself. I realized that I could not love my life either, as I didn't know exactly how I felt about it. I had to dig deep to start paying close attention to what I was feeling, acknowledging and encouraging those feelings. I had never developed the practice of asking myself, "What do you really think about this?" In many ways, I realized, I was a virtual stranger to myself and what my real potential might be and what my future could truly be.

It became increasingly apparent to me that I needed to take responsibility for creating the life that up until then I only had dreamed about. I had not taken personal responsibility to live my life entirely from choice and become the person and the dream activator I truly wanted to be. If I felt sadness, I didn't realize I could intentionally move through it to a different place. If I had a headache, it never occurred to me to write about it, write down to its source, and then eliminate future headaches by writing new conditions into my life.

If I felt victimized, I was unaware that I could write to notice how I had been letting others make my decisions for me and then take control by envisioning and writing a new chapter in my life. Without consciously knowing, as I was writing my way through this first journaling workshop, my life had started to change. In becoming a more confident writer, I became a confident creator of my life. I began to ask myself questions that were buried deep inside of me and discover my answers. If I could create my life through writing, I wanted to stop short at nothing less than celebrating living a life that I dared to dream and embrace joyfully.

Although I have always created and experienced much joy in my life, I wanted to be *joy-filled*. I wanted to live my joy perpetually. What a wonderful awareness to realize that I could release my emotions, heal my body, integrate my experience as wisdom, and choose joy as my state of being out of it all. Journaling led me to realize that joy was mine to choose in every moment, and I could create my own reality.

Journal writing invited me to pay serious attention to my life and make it a daily practice to check in with my being-ness. I needed to learn how I was feeling emotionally and physically, and I often discovered that I lacked necessary information or was being held back by some belief. By noticing and establishing a benchmark in these areas, I easily adjusted to quickly balancing it all. I learned to live life in joy in real-time with an eye to living my future in the same way.

I noticed in my writing what blocked me from resolution and from taking my next steps. It didn't take long to notice not only the importance of journaling to draw out my inner knowingness but also of reading over what I had written. This provided the process of assessing: "What am I learning? When and why did this begin? Who could I talk with or what issue could I tackle to bring me ever closer to greater understanding and clarity?"

Self-inquiry and self-discovery have gifted me with more knowledge about myself than I would ever have absorbed by reading an entire library of books or consulting countless experts. I urge you to trust yourself! The reality is that you will save countless hours and resources asking the opinion of others about who you are, what you want, and what you can do and accomplish when you can simply keep your own journal.

Journaling has been my rock and my foundation upon which to build self-understanding. It became the only method I needed to experience inner peace and joy. The more peace and joy I brought into my own life, my purpose to help others grow through journaling and becoming their own coach became crystal clear.

Try This

As you move into the culminating lap of your current "Discover and Live True to the Life of Your Wishes, Hopes, and Dreams" cycle, here are some questions designed to help with your journey. Write the answers and summarize them in your journal.

1. What makes my heart sing?
2. In what ways has the definition of my wishes, hopes, and dreams changed since I began writing in my journal?
3. What is my current biggest dream?
4. What is the most important thing I have learned about myself from writing in my journal?
5. What new habits can help me realize my wishes, hopes, and dreams?
6. What new beliefs can help make my wishes, hopes, and dreams a reality?
7. What changes have occurred in me from my self-inventory and journaling so far?
8. What remains for me to complete? What is my plan for completing each step I've listed?
9. What issues, situations, and relationships remain that need to be resolved or dealt with so that I can live true to all my wishes, hopes, and dreams?
10. Who are the people who are empowering me to live my wishes, hopes, and dreams?
11. What are the other empowering forces in my life?
12. What is the biggest stretch I've made so far?

13. What additional stretches will I make?
14. What is the most important thing I need to do to keep myself on track regarding realizing all my wishes, hopes, and dreams?
15. What clues can I pick up from my mood or thought patterns to help me notice when I am or am not living true to all my wishes, hopes and dreams?
16. What are the greatest personal rewards I receive from living true to my wishes, hopes, and dreams?
17. What contribution will I make to the world by claiming all my wishes, hopes, and dreams?

As a final exercise, get your journal and go to a quiet place. Set aside as much time as you need to write the story that pictures you living true to all the wishes, hopes, and dreams you have claimed.

Include a descriptive setting that portrays you, your feelings, your environment, and other involved characters. Incorporate all your wishes, hopes, dreams, values, and motivators into your plot. Write a story climax that shows how all the journaling you've done so far has paid off in wonderful ways. Read your dream story to people who are close to you, who support you, and who are aligned with you.

About the Author

Joyce Chapman is a bestselling author, speaker, and professional and personal coach. A pioneer in the field of journal keeping, she provides step-by-step journaling techniques for actualizing wishes, hopes, and dreams to individuals, groups, and companies through her books, newsletters, workshops, training programs, and coaching sessions. She is known for her landmark books *Journaling For Joy, Live Your Dream, Celebrate Your Dream, Notice! & Journal* and *Notice! The Art Of Observation* and their companion workbooks. Her most recent publication, *Raising A Dreamer*, continues her pioneering work in the field of journaling and offers up one of the easiest motivators for journal-keepers seeking new topics and areas of discovery. You can visit her website at www.joycechapman.com and write her at dreams@joycechapman.com.

CHAPTER 39

Journaling and the Pursuit of Happiness

By Susan Borkin

"The journal has been the thread that has served to keep me sewn together when it felt as though my life was coming apart at the seams. Beyond friends, intimate relationships, major lifestyle changes and deep personal loss, it has always been there."

—Susan Borkin

In the last two decades, the field of positive psychology has burgeoned, with many evidence-based studies on happiness and well-being. What does this mean for journal writers? Fortunately, journaling integrates easily and effectively with positive psychology. Journaling prompts, as well as concrete and specific tools for increasing positive emotion, abound. Both journaling and positive psychology can prompt experiences of a flow state, activate personal strengths, and potentially move on from suffering to flourishing.

Researchers in positive psychology, or the study of happiness and well-being, have identified five primary paths to happiness including the following: Positive emotion, Engagement, Relationships, Meaning, and Accomplishments (PERMA). This chapter will focus on two such paths, which I believe will be the most useful for you. First is a life focused on pleasure and positive emotions, while the second point of focus is a meaningful life.

Pleasure and Positive Emotions

Details are the seasoning in the soup of our memories. The concrete and sensory quality of the details, the chance to taste, smell, touch, and feel is what makes your memories rich and powerful.

One of the quickest ways to increase happiness is to learn to savor in the moment. Take a moment to truly taste each sip of your morning tea, each bite of your honey-sweetened toast, smell the air after the first spring rain, hear the birdsong in the early morning. When you are in the moment, stay in the moment, put journaling aside. It is also important to learn how to savor past and future moments through journaling. This is known as *savoring the past* and *anticipatory savoring.*

Savoring the Past

To savor the past, become quiet and close your eyes. Go back to what you remember as one of the happiest or most fulfilling days of your life or any particularly joyful time in the past. Remember the birth of your first child, her impossibly soft skin against yours, her few strands of silky hair, the tears on your partner's cheeks. As each memory comes to you, write it down. You will have the joy of the memory itself and an opportunity to reread and relive what you have written.

Anticipatory Savoring

In anticipatory savoring, think of something you are looking forward to. Picture everything you imagine will happen at that time. Use all your other senses as well. What will this upcoming event sound like? What might it feel like? Will there be scents you associate with the event? Or perhaps you anticipate tasting something wonderful and delicious. You imagine stepping off the plane, a warm moist breeze greets you, the smell of the ocean, and the greenery everywhere you look. Again, journal all the details you are anticipating. You will experience joy in anticipating and be able to reread what you have written at some point in the future.

While savoring may not be the first thing that comes to mind in creating pleasurable moments, a great deal has been written about gratitude to increase positive emotions.

Here Is My Story...

Many years ago, I went away for a long weekend retreat, something I try to do at least once a year. Many small things went wrong, and I started to get seriously grumpy. Finally, like a cartoon version of "Snap out of it," I thought, "I have so many great things in my life!" I grabbed my journal and began a list entitled: *101 Things I Love.*

This is what I started with:
- *Labyrinth walks*
- *Beach walks*
- *Beautiful lodgings*
- *Quiet streams*
- *A really, really good novel that almost makes me cry because the writing is so delicious*

This has now become a cumulative gratitude list, one that can be added to at any point. Simply glancing at this list in my journal makes me smile.

Another spin on the gratitude list is an exercise popular with those in the field of happiness and well-being. It is called by a variety of names, but I like to call it *Three Good Things Plus*. Using your journal, write down three good things that happened to you today or if it's early in the day, from the day before. For example:

- *I really enjoyed the Zoom call this afternoon.*
- *We had the best dinner last night.*
- *I received the most beautiful thank you note.*

Each of the three things I wrote down were in and of themselves good things. But the next step, the *plus* part means I go back to each of the things I wrote down and note what my part was in making this a good thing. For example:

- I really enjoyed the Zoom call this afternoon...*I spoke up and actively participated.*
- We had the best dinner last night...*I specifically spent time looking up recipes and planning the meal.*
- I received the most beautiful thank you note...*I like to take care in getting just the right gift.*

So first, I have the pleasure of the good thing itself. Then I get an extra dose of self-esteem by realizing I am the positive causative factor for each event.

Circle Your Perspective

An additional quick positive emotion exercise that can be done right in your journal is *Circle Your Perspective*. Go to a blank page. In the middle, put a symbol of the thing or person who is annoying you. Then, all over the rest of the page, encircle the positive things in your life—your partner, your kids, grandkids, your home, your hobbies, your friendships. Look back at your original circle, now lost in the abundant circles of good in your life. How does the original annoyance look to you now?

A Meaningful Life

At age twenty-six, I became an orphaned adult. My crisis was practical because being single, alone, motherless and fatherless was overwhelming and scary. This crisis was also a spiritual one because losing not one, but two parents in my mid-twenties had a profound impact on my daily life, my priorities, and my search to find meaning and purpose in life.

Over my adult lifetime in the past fifty years, I have at times heard myself described as intense, and at other times, driven. My friend Janet once described herself as being happy-go-lucky. Happy-go-lucky, I am not. Purpose is critical to my well-being. What I do means something to me. The need to do work that counts, to contribute, to leave behind a legacy matters to me. Perhaps this is why I have been drawn to the work of researcher Laura King.

Best Possible Self

King has created an exercise called *Best Possible Self*. The exercise guides the participant to take some time to imagine their life in the future. In this scenario, one can imagine that they have worked hard and have been successful at accomplishing their life goals. Everything has gone as well as possible. It is as though you have manifested all your life dreams. She then instructs one to write all they have imagined.

Although the instructions for this exercise are straightforward and sound simple, they are not easy. The exercise requires thought, imagination, and dealing with personal feelings. One can repeat this exercise for several days in a row, periodically, or on an occasional basis. Whatever the frequency, it is a powerful and revealing exercise toward finding meaning.

Write Your Own Obituary

Another exercise for finding meaning is called *Write Your Own Obituary* and has some similarities to *Best Possible Self.* Practicing writing your own obituary is a way to examine in yourself, those things you wish to have remembered. In some ways, this can be a challenging, even frightening, exercise to do. It requires, of course, imagining yourself deceased. On the other hand, pretending to write your obituary is also an opportunity to focus on your purpose and reason for living. If this feels far too intense, try beginning with something like this:

> Susan Borkin passed quietly in her sleep during what appears to have been an afternoon nap. Covered with a light blanket, she was found in an unmade bed. Reportedly, dishes were found soaking in the kitchen sink, as though the dishwashing task was meant to be finished at a later time.

In terms of finding meaning, it is said that the two most important moments in your life are when you are born and when you find out why. When looking for meaning, positive psychology offers the tenet that when we are doing what we do best, we are the happiest. One of the most organic ways to become aware of what you do best is to write about it. There are several ways to go about this. List as many moments as you can when you were in a state of flow—time flew by, you were totally focused, any obstacles you encountered seemed to disappear. Or you can list and write about moments where you felt genuinely in the moment, joyous, and happy. You may also ask people who know you well what they consider to be your greatest strengths or when they have seen you at your best. Take notes as you listen. Do you notice any patterns? Are there repetitive themes about what you notice in yourself and what others tell you? Finding your strengths may take a little effort but living a life of meaning is worth the investment.

Journaling is a powerful tool that enhances many of the tenets of positive psychology, happiness, and well-being. In my experience of journaling, I conclude with this thought:

> Journaling has now become interwoven into the very depth of me, a habit without which I would be seriously diminished. I read somewhere once that "habit is like a cable; we weave a thread of it each day and soon it becomes so strong we cannot break it." And in the weaving of the many and varied threads of my life, writing has created a deeply colored, richly textured quilt, sheltering me from the cold outside and creating a warm deep inner life.

Try This

- For many of us, daily journaling is in and of itself a path to happiness.
- Creating rituals around your journaling practice can enhance this feeling of well-being. If you don't already have a journaling ritual, consider finding a special place to write. Bring a favorite photo, shells, rocks, or other elements from nature to this spot. Light a candle or use your favorite mug. Make this space your own so you will look forward to it each day when you write.

About the Author

Susan Borkin, PhD, is a licensed psychotherapist, speaker, and author. An early pioneer in the field of journal writing, she has specialized in therapeutic journaling since 1978. She is the author of *Writing from the Inside Out, When Your Heart Speaks, Take Good Notes, When the Times Get Tough, the Tough Get Journaling*, and award-winning *The Healing Power of Writing*. Dr. Borkin is a global journaling expert and member of the Journal Council for the International Association for Journal Writing (IAJW.org). She is available for keynotes, consultation, and training. Please contact her at Susan@SusanBorkin.com or visit www.SusanBorkin.com for more information.

CHAPTER 40

Journaling for Your Future Self

By Elena Greco

> "I feel as though I were still master of the days I have recorded, even though they are past, whereas those not mentioned in the pages are as though they had never been."

—Eugène Delacroix

My journal is an old friend that has been with me for most of my life, from early adolescence through my current senior years. I've journaled both regularly and sporadically, journaling regularly for long stretches, then sometimes taking a hiatus for months or even years. But I always come back to it. Why? Because journaling is the kindest, most healing, most self-preserving, and self-validating thing I can do for myself. And because my journal is truly my best friend, the wisest one in my company.

Journaling keeps me flowing and going, providing an outlet for emotions and thoughts that might otherwise grind me to a halt. It gives me a safe space to say whatever I feel like—including snarky things to people who irk me so that I can vent without harming relationships. It gives me a chance to reflect more deeply on what's going on in my life beyond the immediate circumstances, if only for a few minutes a day. Although journaling provides enormous benefit to me in the moment, I journal for two people: my Present Self and my Future Self.

The Present Self

Journaling is incredibly healing for my Present Self, wonderfully beneficial in the therapeutic sense. It helps me bring order to my life. It's a great release for pent-up emotions and chaotic thoughts, and almost as good, and often better, than talking to a counselor or a friend.

When I write in my journal, I write *to* the journal. I write to a faceless entity who provides witness to my existence, a confidante who never judges, one who accepts all I have to give it without question or complaint. In it, I can leave my most vile or violent thoughts without causing damage, either to others or to myself. I can leave my sadness, despair, and vitriol without being judged and feel less burdened for doing so. I can be petty and petulant, or profound and transcendent, and sometimes all of those in the same entry.

When the thoughts in my head are swirling, leaving me no room for clear thought, journaling helps me pour the thoughts onto the page so that they no longer affect my clear vision.

When the superficial but often intense emotions sometimes obscure what's happening, journaling helps me gain clarity. When I feel confused or torn about a decision, I journal, and the options become clear, and the solution arises from the murk. Journaling helps me sort out difficult situations.

When I want to hear from my creative self, journaling helps me get to the creative depths, generating ideas that I can then take to the drawing board—or the music rehearsal or the written page.

Best of all, the journal *never* misunderstands me.

All these things and more are plenty of reasons to journal. But there's an added benefit to journaling that you can't get from talking to a counselor or a friend, a benefit you can't get from anyone or anything else.

Journaling can benefit your Future Self, the you who doesn't exist yet, the you who lives in the future.

The Future Self

Journaling is incredibly helpful in the present. But its greatest value might well be in the future.

Reading from past journaling brings back memories and helps me recall what happened. I often forget much of my past until I'm reminded by my journal, and I sometimes have an altogether different memory of past times. Reading the journal brings back those times more realistically, correcting the whims of my memory. When I read past journals now, I'm amazed at the experiences I've gone through in my life in a way that I could not possibly appreciate when they occurred in the present.

Reading past journaling helps me know myself better. I can listen to what I was saying mentally, experience it objectively, and learn from it. My challenging tendencies become clearer so that I can overcome them.

What strikes me most when I read my journaling from a time past is that I sometimes feel compassion for that person—my Past Self—in a way that I couldn't at the time, and maybe in a way that I can't feel for my Present Self in the moment. I listen to that Past Self as a friend in the present; I see and feel her pain and struggles. I feel benevolence for that Self, sometimes suddenly realizing that that person is...me. That helps me feel a little more compassion for myself now, something I often have trouble getting in touch with. Reading the words of my Past Self soothes and heals my Present Self.

Reading my past journals also sometimes allows me to appreciate my positives in a way that I sometimes don't in the present. I see resourcefulness and tenacity, the rising above unfortunate circumstances, and I feel stronger knowing that my Past Self survived and contributed to the current circumstances and strengths of my Present Self.

When I write today, I sense my Future Self lending a benevolent and nonjudging ear, a Self who will benefit from knowing who I am today—my Future Past Self.

Try This

Let's look at how *who*, *what*, *when*, *where*, and *why* can help you get started in journaling or deepen the journaling practice you might already have.

Who. It's a good idea to write to *someone*, whether to an imaginary friend, the journal, your Higher Self, or, maybe, your Future Self. Imagine you're speaking to a Future Self that you don't know yet, but a Self who you know will be wiser than your Current Self and who will have a broader viewpoint, someone who will understand things you can't understand right now. You get to choose who will "hear" your journal entries.

What. The content of your journal posts can be as simplistic and mundane or as deep and profound as you like. It can be "I ate too much yesterday" or "I have a newfound commitment to living the virtues of stoicism." It can be "I had a great day yesterday" or "I am developing a clever plan for ousting my boss." Write one sentence or ten pages. There are no restrictions!

And it can change focus and depth from day to day. It's up to you! Where else in life do you get to make *all* the rules? Your journal can be whatever you decide it will be. And remember, your Future Self will thank you, regardless of what you decide to write.

When. When should you journal? Now! Don't wait another minute. You can journal first thing in the morning, last thing at night, or in the middle of the day. When you journal is not as important as that you have a regular time for journaling.

Make journaling an integral part of your life. We tend to stick with things that are a regular part of our routine and not stick with things that aren't. So decide where in your day journaling works for you and stick with it. This means having a regular time for it, having it follow something that is already a part of your routine, and ensuring it flows naturally with other parts of your routine. If it always follows brushing your teeth, for example, you will always do it. You won't have to think about it; you won't have to look at the clock and say, "Oh, it's time for journaling" or "Oops, I missed journaling so maybe I'll skip it today." It will feel natural, like a normal part of your life.

If you have to decide every single day whether you're going to journal, you won't. It needs to happen without your thinking much about it, much like brushing your teeth every morning. I invite you to think about where journaling might fit naturally in your routine. Then do it!

If you find you still have trouble getting yourself to journal, you might make use of one of the several journaling apps available. The one I use has an option to send me an email on the days and times of my choosing to remind me to journal. I've set it up to send me an email first thing so that it shows up in my morning mail. It politely asks me how I'm feeling, then provides me with a button that takes me straight to the journal, no matter where I am or what device I'm using.

Somehow the app's interface makes it seem okay to write a short journal entry if that's what I want to do that day, so I don't have the excuse that I don't have enough to say to justify journaling that day (a common excuse from people to whom I've suggested journaling). Using an app also allows you to keep your journal private if you're worried about prying eyes, and allows you to download your entries if you want to keep a copy offline.

Where. Another lovely thing about journaling is that you can do it anywhere. All you need is a laptop, a pad and pen, or a smartphone app. You can journal on your train commute, during your break at work, at your desk at home, on a bench in the park, sitting on the beach, or lying in bed. There's no place that isn't perfect for journaling!

Why. In addition to the many reasons above, journaling allows you to know and appreciate yourself more deeply over the years, it helps you to see your life from a broader perspective, and it provides a benevolent partner in life. It gives you a history of your life that you can review at any point to make broad assessments, observe patterns, and give yourself a little credit. Most of all, it is your best friend.

About the Author

Elena Greco is a singer, producer/director, holistic life and creativity coach, and writer. Elena sings both classical and popular genres, performing and recording in New York City. As a producer/director, her primary creative focus is on producing themed multimedia projects that entertain, educate, and enliven. As a coach, Elena helps creatives, performers, and others who want to address creative, practical, psychological, physical, and career issues that impact their life. A former technical writer, she now writes about the creative arts, psychology, communication, persuasion, health, social issues, and politics. She maintains a personal blog and has been published on Kindle and in national publications, including *Psychology Today*, *Thrive Global*, and *Classical Singer*. You can reach Elena at egreco@elenagreco.com or find her on the web at www.elenagreco.com.

Conclusion

"When one person awakens through writing,
the whole world feels this light."

—Lynda Monk

We can't think of a better way to end *The Great Book of Journaling* than with one final journal excerpt and some final journaling prompts!

Excerpt from Lynda Monk's journal, June 26, 2021:

It's 6:00 a.m. I woke early this morning to warm temperatures, unusually so for our area. The current heat wave continues into its second day. I love feeling the warmth of summer while sitting out on our deck sipping my first cup of coffee. A warm breeze is coming off the water and it feels like a wave of goodness for starting this new day. The sounds of geese, eagles and other morning birds are slowly rising too. A hummingbird just visited the small rose flower in our garden box and Sadie is at my feet.

Peter is in his big comfy chair beside me. It is not a deck furniture style chair, but something for a living room or for watching the hockey playoffs. But he is happy in this chair, reclined and relaxed drinking his morning coffee and chatting about our day ahead, so perhaps it is the perfect chair, in the perfect spot. Our boys are asleep in their beds. All feels right in the world.

It's so important to capture the moments that feel perfect and worry free, they are great anchors for more turbulent times. They create memories for settling back into when the world spins hard or sad times our way.

Yesterday morning, I was writing about my deep sadness that Mom is no longer able to answer her phone in her care home room. Alzheimer's is taking her further away from me, from us, from our family. I remember back to the first moment when Dad could not remember who I was, even briefly. Not only did I lose a part of him that day, but I felt like I lost a part of myself too. I can't believe it is almost four years since he died. I can't even recall how many years prior to that it was when he remembered who I am.

I like remembering things as I journal, except for the things I would rather forget.

I am grateful that Covid travel restrictions are lifting soon. As soon as they do, I will get on a plane to be with my mom. I hope it will not mark the first moment I walk into a room, and she does not know who I am, but it might be. It very well might be.

I think I will come back to listening to the birds, sipping my coffee, being here now in the present moment. The place where peace can be found or chosen, most of the time. Back to giving my full presence to the page, to the morning, to the heat against my skin. To my husband beside me. To my pen moving over the page.

Trust Yourself, Trust Your Writing

Have you ever noticed that journaling can often lead to more journaling? The more you write, the more you have to say. Or you start writing about one thing and end up writing about something else altogether? Like this morning, I was writing about enjoying the birds and my coffee, and the next thing I knew, I was writing about both my parents having Alzheimer's disease.

Trust your writing. Trust yourself. Follow the words and your inner and outer world where they want to go; you never know where you might end up. And that unknown journey of self-discovery is one of the main reasons to journal. Over and over again.

Journal Writing Prompts

- What do you want to remember from reading this book?
- What do you want to savor about your day?
- How can you bring present moment awareness into your writing?
- What benefits do you want to experience from your journal writing practice?
- What benefits have you already gained from personal expressive writing?

Final Reflections

The contributing authors in this book have shared up-close and personal accounts of how journaling has benefitted them and even changed them in some instances. This book demonstrates how we can journal in a variety of ways, and we can write to gain a multitude of benefits, including new insights, self-discoveries, and specific life experiences or results through journaling.

We hope you have found something of both value and inspiration for your own journal writing journey in the pages of *The Great Book of Journaling*. Each chapter offers unique journaling methods, various applications for journaling, and personal journaling excerpts from many authors, along with a "try this" section in each chapter.

Journal writing can involve documenting life events and expressing our thoughts and feelings. It can also be a place for asking important life questions. In this way, journaling becomes a valuable companion for making decisions in life, solving problems, and living true to our heart's desires. As Carl Jung said, "To ask the right question is already half the solution of a problem."

What questions do you have at this time in your life? You can simply begin by writing them down and seeing what insights and ideas emerge as you respond in your journal. Allow yourself to be surprised at what inner wisdom flows from you with the help of your personal journaling practice.

In this book, you have learned from some of the world's leading journaling experts, including Lucia Capacchione, Kathleen Adams, SARK, Joyce Chapman, Susan Borkin, Sandra Marinella, Jackee Holder, Judy Reeves, and many others.

We have taken you from juicy journaling to how to deal with journaling resistance. We have explored some journaling basics and what can be found in the richness of journaling simplicity, all the while discovering that the simplicity of journaling can result in significant life-changing and life-enriching results.

You have discovered many different types of journals, including:

- The Reflective Journal
- The Creative Journal
- The Storytelling Journal
- The Healing Journal
- The Legacy Journal
- The Elemental Journal
- The Digital Journal
- The Planning Journal
- The Altered Journal
- The Becoming Unstuck Journal
- The Forest Journal
- The Audio Journal
- The Conflict Resolution Journal
- The Contemplative Journal

You have also explored various ways to use journaling, such as Inner Critic Journaling and Third-Person Journaling, and Keeping the Fragmentary Journal. You have read about writing through the body and journaling as an instrument for mindfulness. You have discovered the power of journaling for yourself and the possibilities of journaling in community with others.

This book offered ideas, prompts, and activities for journaling with children or using it for intergenerational storytelling, creative writing, memoir writing, connecting with nature's wisdom, capturing travel adventures, gaining design inspiration, or finding love. You have learned how to journal for personal growth, finding lost words, dream fulfillment, the pursuit of happiness, and connecting with your Future Self.

As we bring this book to completion, we hope this is only the beginning of your deepened journaling journey and the vast explorations and self-discoveries possible for you through your writing practice. A practice is something we return to repeatedly to know, grow, and care for ourselves. Journal writing helps you listen within and follow the wisdom of your inner voice that wants to be expressed, not only on the page but in your day and in the world.

Journal often, live well.

FREE Journaling Resources

You can find many free journaling resources on the *International Association for Journal Writing* website: https://iajw.org/free-journaling-resources/

You can also access our free *7 Servings of Journal Juice* Gift at http://iajw.org/journalwriting.

Editors' Contact Information

To be in touch with Dr. Maisel, drop him a line at ericmaisel@hotmail.com. Or you can visit him at ericmaisel.com.

To be in touch with Lynda Monk, please connect with her at lynda@iajw.org. You can also visit the International Association for Journal Writing at http://iajw.org.

Acknowledgments

Thank you to all the creative and passionate contributing authors to this book. *The Great Book of Journaling* would not exist without your words and contribution. You are each living proof of the profound and plentiful benefits that journaling can bring into peoples' lives.

Loving gratitude to our supportive spouses, Ann and Peter, and our families, for being our anchors, cheerleaders, and champions in daily life.

A huge thanks to our editor, Brenda Knight, and everyone else at Conari/Mango, especially Morena Guerrero, Robin Miller, and Minerve Jean, who helped make this book a reality.

Thank you to people all around the world who have been participants in our respective journaling and writing offerings. We have had the privilege of supporting and guiding others to write openly and freely, allowing us to regularly witness the transformational power of writing in peoples' lives. This witnessing, in part, inspired the idea to write *The Great Book of Journaling*.

Lastly, our appreciation and acknowledgment to journal writers everywhere. Each time you write, you give something to not only yourself but to others too. For each time one person awakens through journaling, something positive is contributed to the ever-emerging collective consciousness.

About the Authors

Eric Maisel, retired family therapist and active creativity coach, is the author of over fifty books, among them *Redesign Your Mind*, *The Power of Daily Practice*, *Coaching the Artist Within*, *Fearless Creating*, and *The Van Gogh Blues*. He is lead editor for the Ethics International Press Critical Psychology and Critical Psychiatry series and his Psychology Today blog "Rethinking Mental Health" has over three million views. He can be reached at ericmaisel@hotmail.com and you can visit him at ericmaisel.com

Lynda Monk, MSW, RSW, CPCC is a Registered Social Worker, a Wellness Coach, and Director of the International Association for Journal Writing. She is the co-editor of *Transformational Journaling for Coaches, Therapists and Clients: A Complete Guide to the Benefits of Personal Writing*. She is co-author of *Writing Alone Together: Journalling in a Circle of Women for Creativity, Compassion and Connection*. Lynda regularly teaches, speaks, and writes on the healing power of personal writing. She can be reached at lynda@iajw.org and http://IAJW.org

Mango Publishing, established in 2014, publishes an eclectic list of books by diverse authors—both new and established voices—on topics ranging from business, personal growth, women's empowerment, LGBTQ studies, health, and spirituality to history, popular culture, time management, decluttering, lifestyle, mental wellness, aging, and sustainable living. We were recently named 2019 *and* 2020's #1 fastest-growing independent publisher by *Publishers Weekly*. Our success is driven by our main goal, which is to publish high-quality books that will entertain readers as well as make a positive difference in their lives.

Our readers are our most important resource; we value your input, suggestions, and ideas. We'd love to hear from you—after all, we are publishing books for you!

Please stay in touch with us and follow us at:
    Facebook: Mango Publishing
    Twitter: @MangoPublishing
    Instagram: @MangoPublishing
    LinkedIn: Mango Publishing
    Pinterest: Mango Publishing
    Newsletter: mangopublishinggroup.com/newsletter

Join us on Mango's journey to reinvent publishing, one book at a time.

CPSIA information can be obtained
at www.ICGtesting.com
Printed in the USA
JSHW021920270522
26414JS00002B/2

9 781642 508543